"I'm sorry," the doctor finally said. "I'm afraid Helen will be both deaf and blind for the rest of her life."

"So there's no hope?" Mrs. Keller asked in a shaking voice.

"Well, there's still hope that Helen can be taught," the doctor answered. "She seems unusually bright."

"*Taught*?" Captain Keller asked doubtfully. "How on earth can a child who can't see or hear be taught anything?"

Helen Keller
From Darkness to Light

Tanya Savory

 THE TOWNSEND LIBRARY

Helen Keller
From Darkness to Light

TP **THE TOWNSEND LIBRARY**

For more titles in the Townsend Library,
visit our website: www.townsendpress.com

Copyright © 2017 by Townsend Press
Printed in the United States of America

0 9 8 7 6 5 4 3 2 1

Photograph courtesy of Library of Congress
Prints and Photographs Division Washington, D.C.

Townsend Press, Inc.
439 Kelley Drive
West Berlin, NJ 08091
cs@townsendpress.com

ISBN-13: 978-1-59194-501-7

Library of Congress Control Number:
2016957357

Contents

Chapter 1

"Helen! No!"

A frantic Mrs. Keller rushed toward six-year-old Helen as the furious girl grabbed the edge of her doll's crib and rocked it violently. Helen had discovered her infant sister, Mildred, sleeping in the crib. Already jealous of the attention her mother had been giving the baby, Helen completely lost control. In the split second before Mildred went flying out of the crib, Mrs. Keller scooped up the infant.

Helen reached up and pulled at her mother's skirt. When her mother ignored her, Helen growled in fury, grabbed a lamp on a nearby table, and threw it against the wall. The lamp shattered; the startled baby began howling. Helen's hands reached toward an expensive vase, but as her fingers curled around it, she smelled the sweet scent of her favorite candy. Helen's father, Captain Keller, gently wrapped his arms around his daughter and pressed a peppermint candy to her lips. With a greedy snap, Helen bit down on the candy and ran from the room.

"This can't continue," Captain Keller said in a strained, angry voice. "Things are getting worse with Helen. She could have killed Mildred!"

Mrs. Keller rocked and soothed the infant and shook her head. "I don't know what to do," she replied. "How can we make her understand? How can we reach her?"

"We can't," Captain Keller said with a frustrated frown as he began picking up the pieces of the broken lamp. "And we never will," he added gloomily.

"I just can't believe it's completely hopeless," Mrs. Keller said. She sighed as she smoothed Mildred's hair and listened to the familiar sound of Helen repeatedly kicking a locked door somewhere in the house.

It hadn't always been this way.

In 1880, Helen Adams Keller had been born a healthy, normal baby. In fact, as she grew, she seemed to be even brighter and more curious than most babies. At only six months, she asked for water by saying her first word—"wah-wah." Bird songs attracted Helen, and she would gaze for long periods of time up into the branches of the old oak trees that grew in the front yard of the Keller home in Alabama. And bright dancing shadows of leaves on the kitchen floor excited Helen. Before she was one, she took her first steps as she tried to chase the shadows.

But then, when she was a year and a half old, Helen became extremely sick. In the 1800s, babies often died of illnesses that doctors didn't understand and couldn't treat. Baby Helen had a high fever, but other than that, the Keller family doctor had no idea what was wrong. Calling her illness "brain fever," the doctor told the Kellers to prepare for the worst. Helen would surely not make it through the night.

Mrs. Keller sat beside her baby's crib all night, putting her cool hand on Helen's forehead and singing gentle songs to her. Surprisingly, Helen's fever broke in the middle of that long night. In the morning, Mrs. Keller leaned over her baby's small bed and smiled with relief as dawn's pink sunlight streamed over Helen's face. But as the sunlight grew stronger, Mrs. Keller noticed something wrong. Why didn't Helen blink or turn away from the glare of the sun? Didn't the bright light hurt her eyes? Frightened, Mrs. Keller waved her hand in front of·Helen's face. There was no response. She grabbed a lamp and pointed the light directly into Helen's eyes. Helen didn't even move. The terrible realization hit Mrs. Keller as she backed away from Helen's crib.

"Blind!" she cried out as she ran down the stairs in search of her husband. "Our baby is blind!"

But it was even worse than that.

Later that day, as Mrs. Keller held a napping Helen on the front porch, a loud bell rang at the edge of the house, indicating it was time for dinner. The clanging bell startled Mrs. Keller, but Helen continued sleeping peacefully.

"Helen?" Mrs. Keller said loudly. "*HELEN!*"

In a panic, Mrs. Keller grabbed a can of stones that Helen used as a rattle and shook it right by Helen's ear. The baby slept on.

"Deaf, too," Mrs. Keller said quietly to herself as tears filled her eyes.

The Kellers watched Helen closely for several days, hoping that, perhaps, her eyesight and hearing would return once she was completely well. After all, neither they nor their doctor had ever heard of a child losing both her sight and hearing overnight. Was it even possible? The Kellers prayed that it was not.

And the Kellers wondered why Helen, if she could truly no longer see, wasn't terrified and confused. She seemed so calm and slept as peacefully as ever. Years later, Helen would write, "I was too young to realize what had happened. When I awoke and found that all was dark and still, I suppose I thought it was night, and I must have wondered why day was so long in coming. Gradually, however, I got used to the silence and darkness that surrounded me and forgot that it had ever been day."

Finally, the Kellers came to accept that an unheard-of tragedy had struck little Helen. She was both deaf and blind. The beautiful little girl with bright blue eyes, whose very name meant "light," was living in complete darkness and silence.

Over the next few years, the Kellers traveled to many doctors and specialists. Couldn't anything be done? Doctor after doctor shook their heads and sent the Kellers away without hope. Helen was able to communicate in her own limited way. If she wanted her mother, she stroked her own cheek. If she wanted her father, she imitated putting on and taking off glasses. When she wanted ice cream on a hot summer day, she rubbed her arms and shivered. In all, Helen had about 60 signs she used to let her family know what she wanted. But these signs were not nearly enough.

By the time Helen was four years old, she knew she was different in ways that made no sense to her at all. Although she used signs, she realized that other people used their mouths to communicate. Helen often stood between her mother and father and touched their mouths as they spoke to each other. She felt them gesture with their hands while their mouths moved. What were they doing? Helen would move her lips and hands, but nothing would happen. No one seemed to understand her, even though they seemed to understand each other. Sometimes this frustrated Helen so much that she would kick and scream until she wore herself out.

As Helen got older, her temper got much worse. She pinched and slapped strangers when they took her parents' attention away from her. Once, she pulled her grandmother's hair and then ran through the house shrieking and knocking things over when the elderly woman would not let her sit in her lap. And because the Kellers did not know how to teach Helen right from wrong, Helen began to get into all sorts of mischief and trouble. Mrs. Keller, in particular, was reluctant to punish Helen. For one thing, she didn't think Helen could understand what punishment was or why she was receiving it. In addition, Mrs. Keller had no idea how to discipline a deaf and blind child. But most of all, both Captain and Mrs. Keller knew that not letting Helen have her way would lead to an all-out temper tantrum that could last for hours. Helen would scream and kick until she literally collapsed from exhaustion. It was easier just to let Helen run wild.

But things were beginning to get just a little too wild.

One morning, Helen was playing with the Kellers' cook's daughter, Martha. Martha and Helen were about the same age, and because the two girls had grown up together, Martha understood Helen better than almost anyone else. And she was usually happy to help Helen with her "pranks." On this particular morning, Martha was helping Helen cut out paper dolls when Helen suddenly took her pair of scissors and began cutting Martha's hair. Helen motioned for Martha to do the same, so Martha began snipping away at Helen's long blonde curls. By the time the girls were discovered by a horrified Mrs. Keller, they were both nearly bald.

Not long after this, Helen figured out how to lock doors. One afternoon, Helen's mother went into the pantry to get some sugar. Helen sneaked up behind her mother and slammed the door shut. Mrs. Keller didn't think much of this until she heard Helen turn the key in the lock. Knowing that Helen couldn't hear her yelling, Mrs. Keller banged and kicked the door, hoping that Helen would feel the vibrations and release her. For three hours, Mrs. Keller was locked in the pantry. When Captain Keller finally came home, he found Helen sitting outside the pantry door smiling, the key grasped in her hand. The heavier the kicks on the door, the wider her smile became.

These pranks were annoying, but when Helen nearly set herself on fire drying a skirt that had gotten wet in the rain, Captain and Mrs. Keller became worried. And when Helen tried to throw her sister out of the doll cradle, they knew something had to be done—quickly.

"Send her away to an institution," several family members said. "She's clearly got something wrong with her brain. You'll never be able to teach her anything."

Helen's parents would not hear of "sending her away." They knew what this meant. The type of "institution" family members were suggesting was for the mentally ill and the mentally handicapped. They were dreadful places whose residents were often mistreated and ignored. Helen's life in an institution would be, at best, lonely, dull, and dark. It would barely be life at all.

The Kellers took one last chance on a doctor who had a reputation for curing "hopeless" cases of blindness. They had taken Helen to doctors throughout the South, but they made this trip by train all the way to Baltimore. The doctor carefully examined Helen, noticing the signs she made and her reactions to his presence.

"I'm sorry," the doctor finally said. "I'm afraid Helen will be both deaf and blind for the rest of her life."

"So there's no hope?" Mrs. Keller asked in a shaking voice.

"Well, there's still hope that Helen can be taught," the doctor answered. "She seems unusually bright."

"*Taught?*" Captain Keller asked doubtfully. "How on earth can a child who can't see or hear be taught anything?"

"I'm not sure," the doctor admitted. "But there's a gentleman in Washington, D.C., who is an expert on the problems of deaf children. Perhaps he can help you find a teacher for Helen."

The doctor wrote a name and address on a piece of paper. Captain Keller glanced at the name and looked back again in surprise. The name the doctor had written down was Alexander Graham Bell.

Although Bell was mostly famous for inventing the telephone in 1876, he was also a great friend to the deaf, and he was highly interested in developing ways for them to communicate. He had a personal reason for wanting to help those who could not hear—both his mother and his wife were deaf. When six-year-old Helen climbed up onto the famous inventor's knee later that day, the two of them had an instant connection. Helen pulled at Bell's long beard and played with his watch. Bell looked into the little girl's face and felt a great sympathy for her. Her face was not the happy, innocent face of a little girl at all.

"It was chillingly empty," Bell would later recall. There was nothing in Helen's expression that suggested a personality.

"Send a letter to Michael Anagnos at the Perkins Institution for the Blind in Boston," Alexander Graham Bell advised Captain and Mrs. Keller. "He's the director there, and I think he can help you find a teacher for Helen."

Perkins was a different kind of institution. It was nothing like the near-prisons that some of the Kellers' friends and families thought Helen should be sent to. Perkins was a school where the blind learned to communicate, read, and even teach. In fact, a young girl named Laura Bridgman, who was both deaf and blind, had been brought to Perkins 50 years earlier. She had learned to communicate—even to read and write.

Read and write! Mrs. Keller could not believe it! There was hope for her little girl after all. The moment the Kellers returned home to Alabama, they wrote to Mr. Anagnos at Perkins. Could he please send an experienced teacher to Alabama to help Helen? They would be willing to pay the teacher well. And they would be eternally thankful for a teacher who could open up Helen's world the same way Laura Bridgman's world had been opened.

In Boston, Michael Anagnos read the Kellers' letter and considered their request. It was not possible to send a teacher who was experienced in teaching blind *and* deaf children. In fact, Laura Bridgman was the only such child who had ever been taught to communicate. And that had been five decades earlier. Anagnos looked at a list of students who had recently graduated from Perkins, and his eye fell upon one student's name in particular. She had graduated at the top of the class. She was only 20 years old, and she was known to have a temper and stubbornness that was matched only by her brilliance and kindness.

But would she be able to teach Helen? Anagnos wasn't sure. The young woman had learned how to communicate with a deaf child and with a blind child—but not a child that was both. Nevertheless, Anagnos spoke to the recent graduate about the job and encouraged her to take it.

"But I've never taught!" she said with a frown. "I'm not sure I'd even be any good at it."

"I have every faith in you," Anagnos replied. "You'll be wonderful."

"I'll have to think about it," the young woman said doubtfully.

Back in Alabama, Captain and Mrs. Keller waited impatiently for a letter from Mr. Anagnos. Finally, several months later, a reply came. A young teacher, a recent top graduate of Perkins, was on her way. Her name was Annie Sullivan.

"I had gotten used to the silence and darkness that surrounded me and forgot that it had ever been different, until she came," Helen later wrote. "My teacher—who was to set my spirit free."

Chapter 2

Annie Sullivan was tired, angry, and worried. The train she was taking from Boston to the Kellers' small town in Alabama was taking much too long. Somehow she had been sold a ticket for a train that stopped at nearly every station along the way instead of a ticket for the express train. The trip was taking three days instead of one.

Annie squinted at her watch for the hundredth time. Her eyes were very fragile—she had been nearly blind ten years earlier. Now, when she got tired or upset, her vision dimmed. It scared her to even think of going blind, so she leaned back in her seat, shut her eyes, and tried to relax. As the miles and farms and hills crawled by her window, Annie thought about how far she had come in ten years. It hardly seemed possible that she was an educated woman on her way to being a teacher hundreds of miles from her home.

Annie and her brother, Jimmie, the children of an alcoholic father and a sickly mother, found themselves abandoned when Annie was ten and

Jimmie was five. Their mother had died, and their father didn't want to be bothered with them, so the two were sent to the "poorhouse" in a small town in Massachusetts. This was the dreaded place where those who were too poor, young, or sick to take care of themselves ended up. It was a nightmare for Annie the entire time she was there. Later she would write that while in the poorhouse, she "longed desperately to die."

The first night Annie and Jimmie were in the poorhouse, there were no beds available, so they were sent to sleep in a dark room at the far end of the building. The room served as the "dead house." This was the place where those who had died were placed on cots until they could be buried. Annie and Jimmie huddled together in the corner, as far away from the dead bodies as they could get. Rats and mice ran over the children's legs, and the scurrying of cockroaches whispered in the children's ears.

But that wasn't the worst of it.

Jimmie had always had a bad hip, but in the poorhouse the hip became infected. Soon, Jimmie was unable to walk, and fever burned in him. Only a few months after Annie and Jimmie were dumped at the poorhouse, Jimmie died. Suddenly, Annie found herself all alone in the world.

"I believe few children have ever been so completely alone as I was," Annie wrote years later. "I felt that I was the only thing alive in the world. Not a ray of light shone in the great darkness which covered me that day."

And then another kind of darkness began covering Annie. When she was five, an eye disease had damaged her vision. Because the disease had not been treated properly, her vision never returned to normal. And now, bit by bit, her eyesight was growing worse. Soon, she could see no more than shades of colors and blurry movements. Terrified by the idea of becoming totally blind, she begged for any kind of help at the poorhouse, but no one there knew what to do. One day, an older woman told Annie about the Perkins Institution.

"They might take you in there," the woman said with a shrug. "They're always interested in teaching and helping blind children."

Annie couldn't imagine that an important place like Perkins would let a poor orphan in, but she was wrong. Mr. Anagnos and a few other instructors at Perkins met with Annie, and they were impressed by her intelligence, her courage, and her determination. After living in the poorhouse for four horrible years, Annie suddenly found herself in a clean and cheery new home. Perkins paid for an operation that improved Annie's eyesight greatly. She would need to wear dark glasses and not strain her eyes, but otherwise she could see well enough to do almost anything that typical fourteen-year-old girls do.

Six years later, Annie graduated at the top of her class at the Perkins Institution. She was now well educated and understood how both the deaf and the blind learn how to communicate and read. Deaf students used a sign language to "speak," and blind students learned to feel letters with their fingertips for reading. But now as Annie gazed out the window at the changing landscape, she wondered how she would teach Helen. A deaf student could *see* hand motions and letters and books. A blind student could *hear* a teacher explain what words and letters were. But a child trapped in both silence and darkness—that would be something altogether different.

"Miss Annie?" A young man with a strong Southern accent rushed over to Annie Sullivan as soon as she stepped off the train in Alabama. "I'm James Keller, Helen's stepbrother."

At eighteen, James had watched Helen grow up. He thought there was absolutely no chance that Helen could be taught anything. He had hunting dogs that were far better behaved than his stepsister. Now he looked at this young woman and shook his head.

"You were brought here to teach a wild animal," he told Annie with a pitying smile as he loaded her suitcases into the back of a carriage. "Helen can't learn anything."

Annie just nodded, unwilling to make any

judgments about Helen until she had spent some time with her.

When the carriage pulled up in front of the house, Annie saw Helen standing near the front door with a hand stretched out. "Her face wore an eager expression," Annie later recalled. "It was as if she was expecting someone."

After meeting Captain and Mrs. Keller, Annie immediately went to Helen and put her arms around the little girl and tried to kiss her. But Helen drew back and violently pushed Annie away. Annie reached for Helen again, and Helen pinched her and then began kicking. Not until Annie brought out a doll, a present for Helen, did Helen stop resisting. With one arm gripping her new doll, Helen reached up with her other hand and felt Annie's face and hair. Gently, Annie took Helen's hand and spelled D-O-L-L into it, shaping her fingers into the letters that deaf people used to communicate. Helen sat still with her head tilted to one side. What was this stranger doing?

Annie repeated the letters again and again. Then she slowly pulled the doll out of Helen's grasp. Helen stomped and reached wildly for the doll, but Annie grabbed Helen's hand and spelled D-O-L-L again. Then Annie formed Helen's fingers into the letters. When she was done, she handed the doll back to Helen. After repeating this giving and taking of the doll several times,

Helen slowly spelled the letters back into Annie's hand.

"You are a fast little learner, aren't you?" Annie murmured softly.

"She's learned to spell already?" Captain Keller asked in astonished voice from where he had stood watching on the porch.

"Oh, no," Annie was quick to say. "She's simply imitating me. To her, it's just a fun game that means nothing."

"But she's spelling the word back into your hand," Mrs. Keller insisted hopefully.

"She's making a design in my hand," Annie explained. "She has no idea what words or letters are yet."

"How long will that take?" Captain Keller demanded.

"I have no idea," Annie replied with some irritation in her voice. "Clearly, that's what I'm here to find out."

Captain Keller was not used to having a young woman speak to him so directly and without the type of politeness he usually demanded. The woman's Yankee accent and dark glasses made him nervous. He was not about to let a stranger have the upper hand in his household.

"Well, we want to see some progress quickly with Helen," Captain Keller said sharply. "We aren't paying you to play fun games, as you say, with her."

Annie felt her temper rise, but she kept it in check. It would not help Helen at all to argue with her father on her very first day.

"Yes, Captain," Annie said quietly as she handed Helen the doll and quickly spelled the word one more time in Helen's hand before going upstairs to unpack.

Over the next few days, Annie was appalled by the Kellers' complete lack of control over Helen. They allowed her to hit and pinch when she was upset: Helen threw anything within reach across a room when she grew bored or angry. Perhaps worst of all were Helen's table manners—or, rather, complete lack of them. At every meal, she grabbed handfuls of food from serving dishes, tested the food, and then flung it to the floor if she didn't like it. And to Annie Sullivan's utter disgust, Helen was allowed to wander around the dinner table and take whatever she wanted from anyone's plate with her dirty hands.

"Has she never been disciplined at all?" Annie asked Mrs. Keller while Helen threw a screaming fit over finding the door to the stranger's bedroom locked.

"It's just easier to let her have her own way," Mrs. Keller explained. A worried frown wrinkled her forehead as Helen kicked at the door and howled. "She doesn't know any better."

"She doesn't know any better because she's been terribly spoiled!" Annie replied fiercely. "It does her no good to always let her have her way. Can't you see that?"

"Oh, please, Miss Sullivan," Mrs. Keller pleaded as she looked at Helen's face turning purple with rage. "Won't you please just unlock the door for Helen?"

"I will *not*," Annie said as she unlocked the door, quickly walked in her room, shut the door in Helen's face, and turned the lock again.

That night up in her room, Annie paced the floor unable to sleep.

"Obedience is the gateway through which knowledge and love enter the mind of a child," Annie wrote in a letter to a friend that night.

She *must* first make Helen behave if the child was going to learn anything at all. As long as Helen thought she could do as she pleased, she would never settle down enough to be able to learn. Late into the night, Annie thought about how to handle, how to *tame*, this willful spoiled child. Perhaps, Annie finally concluded, Helen had met her match. After all, it had been sheer determination and strength that had pulled Annie through years of hardship, terror, and sorrow when she was a child.

I can be just as determined and stubborn as you, Annie thought as she turned out her light and stared up at the darkness.

The next morning at the breakfast table, Helen made her rounds, reaching toward whatever food she wanted on everyone's plates. She had not grabbed food from the stranger yet, but this morning she could smell sausage on Annie's plate. And that was Helen's favorite food. Slowly, she reached out her hand. Suddenly, a firm grip circled her wrist and pushed her away. Helen was furious. She reached again. Again, she was pushed away. Helen began to growl—a sure sign that a tantrum was coming.

"Just let her have it," Captain Keller said from behind his newspaper. "I prefer not to start my day with hearing Helen screaming."

Instead of letting Helen have the sausage, Annie stood up while holding Helen's arm firmly and said, "I must insist that all of you leave me alone with Helen in the dining room."

Captain Keller was stunned. How dare this brash young woman ask him to leave his own breakfast table! He refused. In turn, Annie refused to back down. Captain Keller's voice rose in anger.

"Helen just wants that one small piece of sausage," Mrs. Keller pleaded, trying to make peace between the two. "Just this once, let her have it. It will be easier."

Annie shook her head firmly. "As long as she is allowed to do as she pleases, she will learn nothing. You may as well send me away this very morning if you want the easy way."

Finally, and reluctantly, the Kellers left Annie alone with Helen, locking the dining room door behind them. What followed was an all-out battle of wills. When Helen realized she was locked alone in the dining room with the stranger, she was afraid at first. Then she lost her temper. Helen threw food, screamed, and broke plates as Annie, again and again, forced her to sit in a chair and eat with a spoon from her own plate. Every time Helen tossed her spoon across the room, Annie dragged Helen over to the spoon, forced it into her hand, and dragged her back to her chair.

Helen pinched and slapped Annie, and Annie pinched and slapped Helen right back. Helen threw gravy at Annie, and Annie grabbed a handful of eggs and dumped them on Helen. Eventually, worn out and very hungry, Helen sat quietly and finished her breakfast with a spoon. Then another battle over using a napkin took place, leading to renewed kicking and screaming. But Helen finally learned to both use and fold her napkin. After two hours, Annie emerged from the dining room with scrambled eggs and gravy in her hair and scratches and bruises on both her arms. She nodded curtly at the astounded Kellers as Helen tore out of the dining room.

"I let her out into the warm sunshine and went up to my room and threw myself on the bed, exhausted," Annie later wrote. "I had a good cry and felt better."

But in spite of all the drama, the first step had been successful. Annie now knew that Helen could be disciplined—as long as her parents were not around to interfere. Annie gazed out her window. Across the yard, maybe 200 yards away, was a small garden cottage that was used mainly for guests when there wasn't enough room in the house. It had its own kitchen and enough room for two people.

Maybe . . . Annie thought. Then she rushed back downstairs.

"What!" Captain Keller exclaimed after Annie explained what she wanted to do. "You want to take Helen out of the house and live alone with her in the cottage? There is absolutely no need to do something so ridiculous!"

"There is absolutely every reason to do it," Annie fired back.

This time, Mrs. Keller supported Annie. She knew that if Annie could not help Helen, there might be no one left who could—or would. After much arguing, Captain Keller finally gave in to his wife's wishes. He admitted that he could see why Annie should be alone with Helen, but he was not happy about the plan.

"You have two weeks to change Helen," he said to Annie Sullivan. "Not one day more."

"But that's not enough time," Annie replied. She glanced outside at Helen, who was repeatedly throwing a watering can against a wall.

"That's all you're getting," Captain Keller said firmly as he turned and walked away.

Chapter 3

Helen sat beside her mother in a carriage, smelling the air and constantly stroking her mother's arm. Where were they going? Helen knew that wherever it was, it was far from home. They had been in the carriage a long time. Helen had been on only a handful of carriage trips that had lasted this long. She was so excited that she couldn't sit still for a moment.

Finally, the carriage stopped, and Helen's mother led her up the steps into a large single room. The space smelled vaguely familiar to Helen, but as she moved around and touched the furniture, walls, and windows, she realized that she didn't know where she was.

"Well, Miss Sullivan," Mrs. Keller said with an uneasy smile, "we've ridden around the farm and fields in a big circle for two hours. Helen surely believes we're somewhere far away."

Annie nodded as she watched Helen move cautiously around the cottage. All the furniture had been rearranged so that Helen would not recognize where she was. Although Helen had been in the cottage quite a few times, she now could not "feel" her way. Frightened, Helen stroked her cheek and reached out her arms for her mother.

"It's time to go," Annie said quietly. Out on the porch of the cottage, Captain Keller watched as Mrs. Keller hugged Helen one last time. The Kellers would be allowed to watch Helen from outside on the porch for the next two weeks, but they could never let her know they were there. Since the main house was only 200 yards away, the Kellers even had to be careful not to cook dishes familiar to Helen. Her sense of smell was so sharp that she could tell the difference between a cherry pie that the Kellers' cook had baked and a cherry pie baked by a neighbor.

Once the Kellers had left, Annie walked over to Helen. She put her arm around the little girl and began spelling words into Helen's hand. By now, Helen knew how to mimic the spelling of several words, and she was always curious about what Annie was doing. But she also feared this stranger who would pinch her back, forced her to use a spoon, and would not let her have her own way. Helen backed away from Annie and reached out for her mother. She felt her way to the door and discovered that it was locked.

She was locked inside a strange place with the stranger!

For nearly two hours, Helen kicked and

screamed. She refused to eat. That night, she crawled underneath the bed she and Annie would have to share and refused to let Annie near her. At some point in the middle of the night, Helen crept into the bed and fell asleep on the very edge, as far away from Annie as she could get.

"I never saw such strength and endurance in a child!" Annie wrote about that first day in the cottage. "But fortunately for us both, I am a little stronger, and quite as obstinate when I set out to be."

Annie would need that strength. Helen continued to fight for days as Annie attempted to tame her wild ways. Hairbrushes were hurled across the cottage. A mirror was shattered. Instead of buttoning up her shoes, Helen threw them at Annie again and again. One morning, Captain Keller stood out on the porch and watched the two engage in a terrific fight over simply putting on a dress. Captain Keller began to wonder if Annie was only making matters worse.

"I have a good mind to send that Yankee girl back to Boston," he angrily told a friend later that day.

But as the days went on, Annie discovered a trick for getting Helen to obey. Helen had become so curious about the patterns Annie constantly drew in her hand that she began holding her hands out for patterns. Annie realized that she could deny Helen the "pattern game" until Helen behaved by getting dressed, eating politely, or brushing her hair. It worked like magic. Helen could not bear being left totally alone. Although she was still somewhat cautious of the stranger, she craved the human contact, and she loved the game the stranger played with her hands.

Within the allotted two weeks, Helen's behavior changed dramatically.

"My heart is singing for joy," Annie wrote. "A miracle has happened! The wild little creature of two weeks ago has been transformed into a gentle child. The great step—the step that counts—has been taken. . . . It now remains my pleasant task to direct and mold the beautiful intelligence that is beginning to stir in the child-soul. Already people remark the change in Helen. . . ."

And, indeed, both Captain and Mrs. Keller were stunned by the change in their daughter. They watched her sit still at the table, use her silverware, and fold her napkin. Every morning, Helen dressed herself carefully and brushed her hair until all the tangles were out. Watching from the porch, the Kellers rejoiced. Annie had succeeded!

"You've done it, Miss Sullivan," Captain Keller said with a smile. "Congratulations on a job well done."

"But I've barely begun," Annie said, startled. "Your daughter is obedient, but she has yet to begin truly learning at all."

The Kellers were confused. They had watched Annie and Helen constantly spell words back and forth in each other's palms. Surely by now, Helen must understand what the spelling meant. They had even seen her spell D-O-G into her dog's paw! But Annie explained that Helen did not yet realize that what was being drawn in her hand were *words* that represented *things*. Perhaps she had spelled D-O-G into her dog's paw, but that was just a coincidence. Annie had also seen Helen spell *doll* and *plate* into the dog's paw.

"How long will it take until she understands?" Captain Keller demanded.

"I don't know," Annie answered honestly. She was puzzled. Helen seemed bright, and she had already learned nearly two dozen word patterns, but the connection wasn't there. Until Helen made that connection, her mind would remain trapped in a dark world of mystery and confusion. The word patterns were no different from Helen's signs for ice cream or for her mother. It wasn't real communication.

In the days that followed, Annie did everything she could to try and break through to Helen, but nothing worked. Annie paced for hours at night and wrote endless letters to friends, teachers, and Mr. Anagnos, asking for advice and help. But "breaking through" to a deaf and blind child was not something that educators knew much about.

"Keep spelling into her hand while she's

touching the object you're spelling," was the main advice Annie received. But she'd already been doing that. Constantly. Annie worried that if Helen did not learn soon, the Kellers would send Annie back to Boston. Captain Keller seemed satisfied enough that Helen was obedient now. But Annie knew that the Kellers would not discipline Helen once she was gone. And Helen would quickly return to her wild ways. Far worse than this, however, was the idea of leaving Helen before reaching her mind. Annie believed Helen was naturally very intelligent, and Annie couldn't bear the idea of leaving that intelligence in the dark.

In desperation, Annie spelled into Helen's hand from morning to night. She spelled until her fingers ached and Helen's palm hurt. Helen was beginning to grasp the idea that making certain patterns in Annie's hand would result in receiving certain things. Making patterns for *doll* or *cake* resulted in Helen being rewarded with her doll or a bite of cake. But Helen didn't realize what words were and how things were words. One word in particular that Helen had trouble with was *mug*. Because water went into her mug, she often spelled *mug* into Annie's hand when she wanted water.

Annie became frustrated. Helen was frustrated, too. One morning, Annie was spelling M-U-G into Helen's right hand over and over again while placing the mug in her left hand. Suddenly, Helen had a rare fit of uncontrolled anger. She yanked her hand out of the stranger's hand, picked up her new doll, and threw it down on the hardwood floor. It shattered into pieces.

"How do I make you understand?" Annie said out loud, her voice shaking with exhaustion and sadness as she swept up the bits of doll. Sighing and looking out the window at the beautiful spring morning, Annie decided it was time for a break. She picked up Helen's mug and handed it back to her, and the two of them headed out to the water pump for a drink of cold water first and then a walk.

Out of habit, Annie continued spelling M-U-G into Helen's free hand as she worked the pump handle. Then as the ice-cold water flowed out of the pump and over Helen's hands, Annie began spelling W-A-T-E-R. Suddenly, Helen's face changed and her body went rigid. Then her mouth fell open with a little gasp.

"She dropped the mug and stood as one transfixed," Annie later wrote. "A new light came into her face."

It was the light of understanding. Perhaps it had been the sudden shock of the cold water that sent that original spark to Helen's mind, but in an instant she understood that *everything had a name*. And all those names had been what the stranger had been drawing in her hand for weeks.

"Everything had a name, and each name gave birth to a new thought," Helen later wrote about that moment. "As we returned to the house, every object which I touched seemed to quiver with life. That was because I saw everything with the strange, new sight that had come to me."

Helen dashed around the yard holding Annie's hand and demanding the name for everything she touched, while Annie cried tears of joy. Helen fell to her knees and pounded on the ground while Annie spelled D-I-R-T. She touched trees, flowers, the garden gate, and her dog, which came bounding toward her to see what all the excitement was about. She demanded the name for everything.

"What has happened, Miss Sullivan?" Captain and Mrs. Keller called from the front porch.

"Come and see!"

The Kellers walked out and took their daughter's hand. Annie wrote M-O-T-H-E-R and F-A-T-H-E-R into Helen's hand, and with trembling fingers, Helen spelled both words back into each parent's hand. The Kellers were overjoyed.

Helen suddenly looked surprised and turned her head to one side. Then she pointed to herself with a funny grin.

H-E-L-E-N, Annie spelled into Helen's hand.

Finally, Helen stroked Annie's arm and

tapped her and nodded.

"T-E-A-C-H-E-R," Annie spelled.

"T-E-A-C-H-E-R," Helen spelled back and threw her arms around Annie Sullivan. The woman she would refer to as *Teacher* for the rest of her life was no longer a stranger to Helen. Most importantly, the world and all the wonders of it were no longer strangers to Helen.

"Before my teacher came to me, I did not know that I *am*," Keller wrote. "I was a phantom living in a no-world. . . . For the first time, I longed for a new day to come."

The "phantom" Helen disappeared remarkably quickly after she discovered that she could, in fact, communicate with those around her. Annie remarked that even Helen's face had changed practically overnight. The "chillingly empty" face that Alexander Graham Bell had been troubled by a year earlier was gone.

"It seems to me there is a sweetness—a soul-beauty in her face which I have not seen before," Annie wrote not long after that miraculous spring morning at the water pump.

During that summer, Helen was so eager to learn new words that she often would not leave Annie's side from dawn until bedtime. She and her teacher wandered through the Alabama fields while Annie constantly wrote the word for everything Helen touched or smelled or felt. Now there was a word for that strange rumbling vibration that Helen had always felt before a rainstorm. The swiftly moving cold water that ran through a small valley past the cornfields had a name. All of it was astonishing and exciting to Helen. She fell asleep making the signs for all these new words in her own hands. By the end of the summer, Helen knew more than 625 words.

But, of course, individual words were not enough. Helen now knew what many words *meant*, but she had no idea how to put them together to form a sentence. She was like a toddler who could say *milk* or *dog* or *play* to indicate what she wanted, but that was all. Annie knew that until Helen could put words together, she would not be truly able to communicate. Annie also knew that most children learn how to talk in full sentences simply by hearing others speak full sentences in conversation. Children learn by imitating what they hear. And, so, Annie began writing full sentences into Helen's hand. At first, Helen was confused, but that didn't last long. With amazing quickness, Helen began putting words, sentences, and ideas together.

Stunned by her student's intelligence, Annie wrote to a friend, "Something tells me that I am going to succeed beyond my wildest dreams."

Once Helen realized that complete sentences were what were happening when people's mouths moved, she was almost too excited to sleep. She demanded constant conversation with Annie.

"She begins to spell the minute she wakes up in the morning and continues all day long," Annie wrote in a letter to Mr. Anagnos at Perkins. "If I refuse to talk to her, she spells into her own hand, and apparently carries on the liveliest conversations with herself."

Soon, Helen had a million questions. "Why does the wind blow?" "Where did the new puppies come from?" "How does a baby robin learn how to fly?" "Who made the shoes that I'm wearing?" Helen's curiosity was so intense that she exhausted herself. Captain and Mrs. Keller worried that their daughter would make herself seriously ill from so much learning.

"But we can't keep her from thinking," Annie explained with a smile. She knew that Helen was far more likely to become sick from being denied learning than from learning "too much."

On Christmas Eve of 1887, a mere six months since Annie Sullivan had arrived to help a wild and uncontrollable little girl, Helen carefully hung her stocking by the chimney. Annie had explained all about Santa Claus and Christmas presents. But Helen was more excited about the presents she was giving to Teacher and to her family than she was about what she might receive. She had written hints into everyone's hands, giggling and then suddenly laughing out loud when no one could figure out what their presents might be.

"She's laughing!" Mrs. Keller gasped and grabbed Annie's hand. "We haven't heard Helen laugh since before she got sick so many years ago. What a wonderful sound!"

Annie smiled and looked at the amazing child who had come so far so fast. She knew there was much more in store for Helen. But even Annie, who always expected the most from her young student, had no idea just how incredibly much more that would be.

Chapter 4

"**D**o you want to learn how to read?" Annie spelled into Helen's hand one cold winter morning not long after Christmas.

A glow and then a wide smile spread over Helen's face. She knew what books were. She had often crawled onto her parents' laps and felt their hands holding something square filled with pieces of paper. Books used to make her extremely angry, because they took her parents' attention away from her—sometimes for hours. In a rage, Helen had thrown more than one book across a room and then picked it up and ripped out its pages.

But Annie had explained that books were incredible little containers of information, stories, dreams, and imagination. Annie had even read books into Helen's hand while Helen sat absolutely still, in awe of the thrilling tales she was taking in. Only when Annie's eyes grew too tired to read anymore would Helen let her teacher close the book. Sometimes Helen found it hard to fall asleep as she thought late into the night about what might happen next in an especially exciting story.

"How can I read?" Helen spelled quickly as she patted her teacher's arm eagerly.

Annie sat Helen down at a desk and put a large card in front of her. On this card were little raised bumps that represented all 26 letters of the alphabet. Helen ran her fingers over the letters and shook her head in confusion. What were these? Annie took Helen's left hand and slowly ran it over the letter A. In Helen's right hand, she made the symbol for the letter A. Helen frowned. This didn't make any sense. To her, the patterns made into her hand to represent words were simply that—just patterns. Just as any child who has not yet learned to read, the concept of letters was brand new to Helen.

Annie did not take time to explain. She simply continued the process all the way through the alphabet, and again, from A to Z. Then Annie spelled a simple word into Helen's hand and then ran Helen's fingertips over the three letters that spelled the word. Suddenly, Helen smiled and nodded. She understood quickly. By the end of the day, Helen knew all the letters of the alphabet, but it would take her (just like any child) time to learn how to spell words. Bit by bit, she began learning spelling using this Braille system, named after the man who had invented it.

Within a month, Helen was able to read complete sentences on the large cards of Braille that Annie used for teaching her.

"Are there books for me?" Helen asked excitedly when she had worked her way through all of the cards.

Annie brought out a number of storybooks in Braille for Helen, but she explained that Braille books were not readily available in most places. At the Perkins Institute, there were hundreds of Braille books for the blind students; but in rural Alabama, books for the blind did not exist. Instead of being disappointed, Helen was thrilled to have even a handful of her very own books. She read them over and over.

"Books tell me so much that is interesting about things I cannot see," Keller wrote several years later. "And they are never tired or troubled like people."

As soon as Helen could read, Annie taught her how to write. Writing came quickly to Helen since she understood letters and words so well. Annie used a system for teaching writing to Helen that blind students used at Perkins. Paper was placed over a wooden board that had grooves in it for letters. Helen guided her pencil along the grooves to make letters for words. Helen could hardly believe that she could now write—just like authors of books! After practicing her writing for a few weeks, she decided she wanted to write a letter to Alexander Graham Bell. She now knew all about the famous Mr. Bell whose lap she had sat upon and whose watch she had played with barely a year earlier. Helen couldn't wait to show Mr. Bell what she could do now.

> *Dear Mr. Bell,*
> *I am glad to write you a letter. Father will send you a picture. I did go to see you in Washington. I did play with your watch. I can read stories in my book.*
> *Good-bye,*
> *Helen Keller*

In Washington, D.C., Bell was beyond impressed—he was amazed. He wrote to Mr. Anagnos at Perkins and asked if he realized how far Helen had come in such a very short time.

"Oh, yes," Anagnos replied. "Miss Sullivan has been writing to me constantly about Helen."

And, in fact, Mr. Anagnos had been writing articles about Helen for publications in Boston and beyond. Already, many people knew about this "miracle child" who had been drawn out of her dark world in barely a year and could already read, write, and communicate with others. At just seven years old, Helen Keller was becoming famous. But in Alabama, neither Helen nor Annie knew anything about this newfound fame as they continued working together.

However, Helen's early education rarely felt like "work" to her.

"For a long time I had no regular lessons," Helen later wrote. "Even when I studied most earnestly, it seemed more like play than work. Everything Miss Sullivan taught me she illustrated by a beautiful story or poem . . . She never nagged me with questions to see if I remembered the day-before-yesterday's lesson. She made every subject so real that I could not help remembering what she had taught."

Annie Sullivan, who had been so worried about failing as a teacher, turned out to be unusually gifted. Like many great teachers, she simply taught the way she liked to learn. So when weather permitted, nearly all of Helen's "lessons" took place outside. Helen held frogs, crickets, and even snakes to learn about different kinds of skeletons. She felt burst cotton-bolls and discovered the tiny seeds in their center when learning about how plants grow. She held an egg in her hand and felt a tiny fuzzy chick hatch from it. And one warm afternoon, Helen and Annie waded along the banks of the Tennessee River, touching the stones, rock, and mud. At one spot, Helen ran her hand up a rocky wall and was surprised at how the texture of the rock changed the higher her fingers reached. She didn't even realize she was having a geology lesson.

Perhaps the only subject that Helen didn't particularly like was math. But her struggle with math made her aware of something else.

Think, Annie wrote into Helen's hand as Helen frowned over a difficult subtraction problem one morning.

Up until this point, Helen had not completely understood words that were not real things that she could touch, like a book or an apple. Words that were ideas or feelings, such as *love* and *think*, were hard for Helen to grasp. But Annie spelled *think* again while tapping Helen on the head. All of a sudden, Helen realized that the focused, difficult feeling in her head that helped her understand things was "thinking"!

But what was "love"? Annie often told Helen that she loved her. What did that mean?

Annie took Helen's hand and patted it on her heart. But that only confused Helen more.

"Love is like the clouds that were in the sky before the sun came out," Annie explained. "You cannot touch the clouds, you know; but you feel the rain and know how glad the flowers and the thirsty earth are to have it after a hot day. You cannot touch love either, but you feel the sweetness that it pours into everything. Without love you would not be happy or want to play."

Years later, Helen still recalled Teacher's explanation.

"I felt that there were invisible lines stretched

between my spirit and the spirits of others," she wrote. "The beautiful truth burst upon my mind!"

And during this time, Helen's mind was opening rapidly. Soon, her reading and writing abilities were far better than those of most children her age. She had learned in nine months what it often takes nine or more *years* for other children to learn. Annie wanted to be careful, though. She made sure that Helen also had the same fun experiences that any seeing and hearing child would have. And Annie didn't believe in limits for Helen. The two of them rode horses through dewy morning fields, zoomed down a steep hill on a sled after a rare snowfall, and sailed in swift sailboats on the river.

Mrs. Keller often worried that Helen was overdoing it or that some of these new experiences might frighten Helen, since she could not see or hear.

"But Helen doesn't seem to be afraid of anything," Annie pointed out. "She's no more fearful of new and exciting things than a normal child might be. Not being able to hear or see is all Helen's ever known. Her condition doesn't make her more likely to be scared."

Years later, Helen could recall only one time when she had been truly afraid. One warm morning, she and Annie took a long walk that passed by a huge old oak tree. The tree had many low-hanging limbs and was perfect for climbing. Annie had helped Helen climb up a small fruit tree on their farm once, but Helen had never been in a big tree. Carefully, Annie helped Helen up to a limb that was wide enough to sit upon comfortably.

"Do you want to have a picnic lunch here in the tree?" Annie spelled into Helen's hand.

Helen nodded eagerly. She loved picnics, and this would be something brand-new. She could feel the big branch swaying gently in the slight breeze, and the smell of early summer blew through the leaves.

"Stay right here and don't move," Annie spelled. "I'll be back with lunch soon."

Helen sighed happily and leaned back against the curving branch. It was so warm that she almost got drowsy while waiting for Annie to return. Then, suddenly, a cool breeze replaced the warm air, and Helen knew the sun had gone behind a cloud. That didn't bother Helen, but what happened next did. A smell came up from the ground that Helen knew well—it was the scent of a thunderstorm. Helen gripped the tree as breezes turned into strong wind. Then a heavy vibration rumbled through her. Thunder!

Helen felt a strange panic flood through her. She knew that thunderstorms could be dangerous if you got caught in one outside. How much more danger was she in, high up in an oak tree?

Overhead, a branch snapped, and Helen could feel the twigs falling on her.

Teacher! Teacher! Helen signed frantically with her hands in the air. But no one was there. Should she jump? How high was she? Would the jump hurt? At that moment, the familiar arms of Teacher wrapped around Helen and lifted her off the branch. In reality, Helen had been only about five feet above the ground. But that experience was a bitter reminder to Helen that no matter how fearless she may be, she was so often completely helpless—and always would be.

In the late spring of 1888, Annie Sullivan received a letter from Mr. Anagnos at the Perkins Institution. He wanted Annie and Helen to come and visit Perkins in Boston for several weeks. He enclosed articles that he had written about Annie and Helen, and he told Annie that people all over the United States now knew about the two of them. He had called Helen "The Eighth Wonder of the World" and a "phenomenon" who was surely a miracle specially sent by God. Now people everywhere wanted to meet this amazing little girl and her teacher.

Annie read and then reread the letter and frowned. She was glad that Mr. Anagnos was pleased with Helen's progress, but she was uncomfortable with him presenting Helen as something amazing and phenomenal. Helen was not some sideshow attraction at the circus! In Annie's mind, Helen Keller was simply a very bright little girl. Of course, she was different from other children, but Annie's hope was that Helen's learning and intelligence would, in time, help her feel *less* different, not *more* different. How could she feel less different if she was put on display for people to gawk at?

Still, there were so many things Helen could experience on a trip like that, Annie thought. And at Perkins, Helen could meet other children her age who were blind. Also, there were all those Braille books . . .

"But she's too young to travel that far!" Captain Keller argued when Annie told the Kellers about Mr. Anagnos's invitation.

"I would be at her side at all times," Annie said. "And there would be so many new opportunities for Helen."

Across the room, Helen sat still. She could tell something was going on. She could feel her father pacing, smell her mother's perfume, and sense Teacher tapping her foot. Teacher did that when she was worried or impatient. The three adults must be talking about her. Helen waved her hand to get their attention.

"What are you talking about?"

Annie came to Helen's side and took her hand. She explained about the letter and the invitation to visit Perkins for a month or so.

"Let's see what Helen says," Mrs. Keller said. "If she wants to go, I think it would be good for her."

Slowly, a smile filled Helen's face. She remembered what Annie had told her about Perkins.

"Will they let me read the books there?" she quickly asked Annie.

"Of course."

That was all young Helen needed to know. She couldn't wait to go to Boston. Years later, she would look back on her time at Perkins and write that the books she read as a child "opened for me magic windows through which I still look upon the universe and find it many-splendored."

Chapter 5

"We went to see Mr. Cleveland. He lives in a very large and beautiful white house, and there are lovely flowers and many trees and much fresh and green grass, and he was very glad to see me."

Helen wrote a letter home to her parents as she and Annie traveled up to Boston in May of 1888. The two of them had made a stop in Washington, D.C., at the request of "Mr. Cleveland"—the president of the United States!

Helen could not quite understand why the president would want to meet her, but she was happy to meet him. And President Cleveland was even happier to meet Helen. He had heard so much about the little deaf and blind girl from Alabama. In 1888, most people assumed that deaf or blind people were not very smart. They believed that the lack of sight or hearing affected the brain, and that those who could either not see or not hear would never be able to learn much. Certainly, someone who was both deaf *and* blind would be completely helpless!

Even President Cleveland admitted to mistakenly believing these false ideas. Helen proved him wrong. The president was both charmed and impressed by this polite seven-year-old who was far from being helpless. In fact, Cleveland could not believe how much Helen *could* do. In many ways, she seemed wise far beyond her years as she took her time to touch and smell the flowers in the White House gardens and comment on them through Annie.

While in Washington, Helen and Annie also visited Alexander Graham Bell. Although Helen had written a letter to Bell about the first time she had met him a year and a half earlier, she couldn't really remember that meeting. She had been her "phantom" self—unaware of even her own existence. Thoughts were not really formed, and memories were vague and easily forgotten. However, Helen had heard a great deal about Bell and was excited to meet him. Bell took Helen's hand and communicated with her for a long time, never taking his eyes off her face. He saw no trace of the "chillingly empty" face he had seen when he first met Helen. Annie also found herself drawn to Bell, whom she described as having "a happy way of making people feel pleased with themselves." The two would remain lifelong friends.

Once at the Perkins Institution, Helen, for the first time in her life, was able to communicate with children her own age.

"What a joy to talk to other children in my own language!" Helen later wrote. She was overwhelmed with happiness by all the blind children who gathered around her, took her hands, and talked nonstop with her about everything from dolls to books to puppies. "They were so happy and contented, that I lost all sense of pain in the pleasure of their companionship."

Perhaps the only person who was not impressed by Helen was Laura Bridgman, the deaf and blind woman who had learned to communicate 50 years earlier at Perkins. Helen was eager to meet someone like herself, but Bridgman, now middle-aged, thought Helen was too much of a tomboy. The older woman definitely did not approve of girls who climbed trees, rode horses, and even sat on the floor to play games! Making matters worse, when Helen bent to kiss Bridgman hello, she stepped on her toes.

During her stay at Perkins, Helen could often be found in the library. She could barely believe how many books were gathered all in one place—and every book was in Braille. She could read every one! She ran her hands along the row after row of books and giggled. It seemed too good to be true.

But Helen certainly did not spend all of her time in Boston reading. She and Annie and Mr. Anagnos visited Bunker Hill, where Helen learned her first lesson about the Revolutionary War. On another day, they visited Plymouth Rock, where the first Pilgrims had landed more than 250 years earlier. Helen walked solemnly over to the rock, knelt down, and ran her hands over its rough surface. A curious, yet serious, expression crept across her face.

"I was interested in the great rock on which the Pilgrims landed because I could touch it, and perhaps that made the coming of the Pilgrims and their toils and great deeds seem more real to me," Helen later explained. As it was with so many things, Plymouth Rock became real to Helen when she could put her hands on it. Helen also smelled the Atlantic and felt the ocean wind on her face. These sensations fired her imagination about the first Pilgrims as much as seeing the ocean and hearing the wind might have excited those who see and hear. Perhaps more!

Near the end of Helen's visit at Perkins, Mr. Anagnos asked her to be a special guest of honor at the school's graduation ceremonies. He invited Helen and Annie to sit on the stage as the graduates came up to receive their diplomas. Not only that, but Mr. Anagnos asked Helen if she would like to present a favorite poem or piece of writing. Helen was so excited she could barely wait for graduation day. She thought of everything she had read and everything she loved. Finally, she chose a poem about birds. These little creatures stirred Helen's heart so much that

Annie had given Helen a pet canary at Christmas.

"My cup of happiness overflowed," Helen later wrote about the canary, recalling how the tiny bird perched on her fingers and ate cherries out of her hand.

Fearlessly, and with a wide smile on her face, Helen stood in front of the large room full of graduates, family, professors, and even the governor of Massachusetts. She used one hand to read the poem in Braille and her other hand to form the words into Annie's hand. Annie then recited the poem out loud. The room was absolutely quiet. No one had ever seen anything like this! By the time Helen was finished, tears filled the eyes of nearly everyone present. Even the governor had to pull out his handkerchief and wipe his eyes.

After graduation was over, it was decided that Helen and Annie would spend the next several weeks of summer at Cape Cod, a popular seaside vacation area just north of Boston. Although Helen had been near the ocean, she had never touched ocean water or felt waves. She was so thrilled that she ran straight into the ocean as soon as she and Annie reached the beach.

"The motion of the water filled me with an exquisite, quivering joy," Helen remembered. "But suddenly my ecstasy gave way to terror. . . . The waves seemed to be playing a game with me, and tossed me from one end to another."

Helen finally came sputtering and coughing out of the ocean, shaking water out of her ears and spitting. Annie ran over to Helen and put her arm around her shoulder. She worried that Helen was afraid and that she might begin to cry.

But Helen simply sat down on the sand and caught her breath. Then she licked some water off her lips and spit again.

"Who put all the salt in the water?" she demanded to know with a grimace. Annie laughed out loud and hugged Helen.

When Helen returned home to Alabama that fall, she thought she had seen it all.

"I thought of Boston as the beginning and the end of creation," she remembered. "I could not convince myself that there was much world left."

However, Helen's discovery of the big world around her was just beginning. As her mind and her curiosity grew, Helen asked Annie to read more and more books to her. Some of the stories took place on top of faraway mountains or on ships upon oceans thousands of miles away or in strange forests full of exotic animals. For Helen, imagination was a delicious treat as incredible as the richest ice cream or the sweetest candy. She often felt as though she were right there in the middle of a story.

"It was a time when I lived myself into all things," Helen remembered.

As a result, Helen could not bear it when Annie put a book down just as the story was getting exciting.

"You have to finish!"

"I cannot. My eyes are too tired," Annie would reply more and more often. Although Annie had had operations to help her eyes years earlier, the pain was now beginning to bother her again. Finally, in the spring of 1889, Annie decided to travel alone to Boston for a few months in order to meet with doctors and have more operations. Helen was devastated.

"How will I live without you?" Helen asked in tears. For more than two years now, Annie had constantly been by Helen's side. They had rarely been apart for more than a few hours.

"You will find plenty to do," Annie reassured Helen. "It will soon be summer!"

Annie had barely been gone five days before Helen wrote a sad and desperate letter to her teacher.

"I want you to come to me soon. I miss you so very, very, very much. I cannot know about many things when my dear teacher is not here. I send you five thousand kisses, and more love than I can tell . . ."

However, in spite of all her dramatic despair, Helen managed to live without Annie. And she had a wonderful summer with her family and many friends at a cabin situated atop a nearby mountain. Cool breezes blew across Helen's face, and unusual scents of wild grapes and tangy cedar trees came through her window every morning. Along with friends who watched out for her and helped her, Helen hiked up and down the mountain and along the nearby river.

One afternoon, however, Helen and her friends became lost. And evening was coming on quickly.

"It's no use," an older boy said as the group stopped at a lookout point on the mountain. "I don't recognize anything around us."

"But look!" another friend said. "There's the train trestle! We can cross it to get back home."

The trestle, a type of wooden bridge, reached across a very deep canyon.

"We would have taken any way rather than this. But it was late and growing dark, and the trestle was a shortcut home," Helen later wrote. "I had to feel for the rails with my toe. I was not afraid . . . until all at once there came a faint 'puff, puff' from the distance."

Helen could not hear the train, of course, but she could feel the vibrations of the approaching train as it rattled the trestle. Far, far below, the river rippled by—but it was much too far to jump. Helen felt hands and arms helping her. At the last minute, the children scrambled down to the crossbeams just beneath the train tracks. The train rushed over Helen's head. She would always remember the blazing heat of the engine as it flew by and the choking smell of the smoke and ashes. If Helen had been concerned about having a dull summer without Annie, she need not have been worried.

When Annie returned to Alabama that fall, her eyes were much better—and she had exciting news. Mr. Anagnos wanted Helen to return to Boston and to Perkins and become a fulltime student every year! It was very hard for Captain and Mrs. Keller to think of Helen being gone every fall and winter, but they knew she had to go. Helen's appetite for books, learning, and new experiences kept growing every day. At barely nine years old, Helen had already far outgrown the small town where she lived. In September, the Kellers gathered once more at the train station to wave farewell to Helen and Annie.

Back at Perkins, Helen took full advantage of everything available to her. She took art classes and learned how to make pottery. In the music room, she put her fingertips on a violin and felt the music vibrate through the smooth wood and into her body. Her hands touched the throats of the blind children in the school choir, and she felt singing. In the science room, there were hundreds of specimens of dried and stuffed animals. Helen touched a fox, an owl, and even the thick fur and sharp claws of a bobcat. Although she had read about these creatures in books, they didn't become real until she felt them. It was Helen's way of seeing them.

And when Helen learned to read and write French in barely three months, Mr. Anagnos was stunned.

"She is the queen of precious and brilliant children," Anagnos wrote in articles that made their way around the world. Now, in places as far away as Japan, people were curious about Helen Keller. Many people began traveling to Perkins in hopes of meeting this famous little girl. But Annie was careful not to let strangers interfere with Helen's education and distract her. Annie often became very angry with Mr. Anagnos. She felt that he was taking advantage of Helen's intelligence in order to make the Perkins Institution and himself famous.

"I would rather be shot than gratify the curiosity of a news-loving public!" she wrote in a furious letter to a friend. Annie respected Mr. Anagnos and everything he had done for blind students at Perkins, and Mr. Anagnos admired Annie's intelligence and fiery personality. But the two often did not see eye to eye when it came to Helen. However, somehow the two of them managed to work out their differences in the best interest of their now-famous pupil.

Unaware of her fame and her teacher's irritation with it, Helen kept busy, always looking forward to achieving new things. One afternoon, Helen learned about a girl who lived in Norway who was also deaf and blind. Like Helen, this girl had also been unable to speak. But after much work and careful training, the Norwegian girl could now talk. She was no longer "dumb" (the word used in those days to describe those who couldn't speak). Helen couldn't believe it! Did this mean that being blind and deaf did not necessarily mean having to be dumb, too? That evening, Helen was unusually quiet. She barely wrote in Annie's hand at all. Annie could tell Helen was thinking hard about something.

Finally, just before bedtime, Helen took Annie's hand and began to write.

"I want to learn how to talk. I know I can do it."

Chapter 6

"**B**ut I have no idea how to teach you how to talk," Annie explained to Helen again the next morning.

Helen just shook her head and tugged on Annie's sleeve, meaning that she would not take no for an answer. Teacher had taught Helen nearly everything she knew. Helen would not accept that she could not also teach her to speak.

Annie frowned and pulled away from Helen. She knew how desperately Helen wanted to talk. Annie had often watched Helen touch others' mouths as they spoke, wrinkling her forehead in concentration and confusion. Then Helen would touch her own mouth and try pushing her lips into the same positions. Once she had done this, Helen would try making a noise. What came out was a weird grunt or sharp shriek that startled anyone nearby.

Deaf people could be taught to speak, but they had the huge advantage of being able to see exactly how the lips and mouth and tongue move when words are spoken. In addition, they could watch themselves in a mirror as their own mouths formed words. But a deaf and blind person? If Annie had not also read about the unusual girl in Norway who could speak, she would not have believed it was humanly possible. She thought it would be too difficult for Helen.

"And the voices of deaf children are not agreeable to me," Annie admitted in a letter. Still, Helen insisted on learning. If Annie wouldn't teach her, could another teacher be found? Reluctantly, Annie visited a nearby school for deaf children and found that the principal, Sarah Fuller, was very willing to teach Helen. Fuller had no experience teaching a deaf student who was also blind, but she was willing to give it a try.

Helen couldn't wait to begin her speaking lessons. Her thoughts and ideas were coming so quickly now that her hand signs for words couldn't keep up with her. Although many of the blind children at Perkins knew the hand sign language, and were able to talk with Helen, she knew, of course, that they spoke to one another much more quickly with their mouths. She wanted to talk to her friends, too! And so her lessons with Miss Fuller began.

Years later, Helen said of learning to speak that "nothing that I have ever accomplished has cost me so dearly in time and effort." Helen had to spend hours and days touching the mouth and throat of her speech teacher and then attempting to make sounds herself. Sometimes Helen even had to put her fingers inside Miss Fuller's mouth to understand how the tongue moved when pronouncing a word. Helen worked until her throat became sore and swollen, repeating a single word or sound hundreds of times.

Finally, Helen was able to speak slowly and awkwardly. Her first sentence was, "It is too warm." Annie and Miss Fuller cheered and congratulated Helen, but in reality, Helen's "speaking" was nearly impossible to understand.

"Her voice was to me the loneliest sound I have ever heard," a friend would later write. "It was like waves breaking on the coast of some lonely desert island."

Even so, during that winter at Perkins, Helen continued to work very hard on speaking. She was determined to greet her family at the train station with words when she returned to Alabama that spring.

"I am not dumb now!" Helen repeated again and again on the long train ride home. Annie squeezed her arm in encouragement. When Helen stepped off the train and spoke these words to her parents, they were stunned. They had had no idea that Helen was trying to learn how to talk.

"My eyes fill with tears now as I think how my mother pressed me close to her, speechless and trembling with delight, taking in every syllable I spoke," Helen later wrote.

However, in spite of all her hard work, Helen's speaking voice would never be very good. Although Sarah Fuller had meant well, she had not taught Helen correctly. Helen would later discover (when it was too late to change) that she should have been taught to make sounds first and then learn how to form words with her mouth. Looking back many years later, Helen said that not being able to talk well was her only real regret in life.

In her second year at Perkins, Helen faced another difficult challenge. Now 11 years old, Helen had become more and more interested in writing. She particularly loved fairy tales, and she began doing some "storytelling" writing of her own just for fun. Annie suggested that Helen write a story for Mr. Anagnos for his birthday in November, and Helen happily agreed. She walked out into a chilly November afternoon and smelled the sharp scent of fall leaves and felt the sting of a frost on its way. She sat for a while and recalled all the descriptions she had read and been told about the beauty of a late fall day.

That evening, Helen wrote a short story about imaginary frost beings who come to change the color of the leaves and then change the seasons. She titled her story "The Frost King," and presented it to Mr. Anagnos along with a birthday card. Mr. Anagnos read Helen's story several times. Helen always amazed him, but this was something altogether different. Her writing skill and imagination was far beyond that of any eleven-year-old he had ever known. Mr. Anagnos quickly published Helen's story in a number of magazines and newspapers.

Almost immediately, several letters arrived at Perkins claiming that Helen had stolen the story. Another story titled "The Frost Fairies" had been written years earlier by an author named Margaret Canby. Helen's story, the letters pointed out, was almost exactly like Canby's.

"I little dreamed how cruelly I should pay for that birthday gift," Helen later remembered.

Neither Helen nor Annie ever remembered reading "The Frost Fairies." There was not a copy of it Perkins, and Annie was positive she had never owned the story or read it to Helen. Helen strongly denied copying the story, and she was hurt to think that total strangers were writing letters to Mr. Anagnos accusing her of stealing someone else's work. And yet the two stories were so similar that even Mr. Anagnos did not believe Helen. As a result, he forced Helen to face a panel of teachers and officers from Perkins and answer their questions. Making matters worse, Annie was not allowed to be with Helen during the questioning. Mr. Anagnos believed that Annie had encouraged Helen to steal the story and was now trying to cover it up.

The teachers asked question after question.

"Are you lying?"

"Do you think it's right to steal?"

"Have you stolen any other writing?"

Helen was terrified.

"The blood pressed upon my thumping heart," Helen remembered. "I could scarcely speak. . . . As I lay in bed that night, I wept as I hope few children have wept. I imagined that I should die before morning."

Alexander Graham Bell heard about what had happened and became very angry—but not at Helen. He never doubted Helen or Annie for a moment. He believed that it was quite possible that Helen had heard the story when she was younger and had somehow stored the wonderful details in her head. Rather than stealing someone else's writing, Helen had simply drawn upon a distant and beautiful picture in her mind. After all, because Helen could not see or hear, she stored memories and "images" differently than most people.

Bell took it upon himself to investigate the matter. After much discussion with Annie and many letters written to various people, Bell got to the bottom of the mystery. Three years earlier, when Helen and Annie had spent a month at Cape Cod, Annie had left for a few days for a brief vacation alone. During that time, the woman looking after Helen (who could also communicate through hand signs) tried to entertain Helen by reading whatever children's books she could find in the house where they were staying. One of those books contained the story "The Frost Fairies" by Margaret Canby!

Helen had been restless and bored during Annie's absence, and she did not particularly enjoy the other woman reading to her. The story did not capture Helen's imagination, and there were so many words in it that she didn't understand. However, even if the story did not interest Helen, the unknown words did.

"I cannot help thinking that I made a great effort to remember the words," Helen would later explain. "One thing is certain. . . . the language was stamped upon my brain."

She had no memory of the actual story of "The Frost Fairies," but Bell had been right—the details had somehow stuck in her head.

Most of the teachers at Perkins apologized to Helen, and even the author of "The Frost Fairies" sent a letter to Helen. "Some day you will write a great story out of your own head," Margaret Canby wrote. But Helen was terribly shaken up by the whole incident, and decided to never again "make up" a story.

"I have never played with words again for the mere pleasure of the game," Helen wrote many years later. "I have ever since been tortured by the fear that what I write is not my own. For a long time, when I wrote a letter, even to my mother, I was seized with a sudden feeling of terror, and I would spell the sentences over and over, to make sure I had not read them in a book."

When Helen returned to Alabama that summer, she was sad and distant. She felt betrayed by Mr. Anagnos, who had gone so far as to call Helen "a living lie" in spite of others' belief in her. She did not want to return to Perkins in the fall. Making matters worse, because Helen and Annie had returned to Alabama and were no longer in the public eye, newspapers around the country began making up stories about Helen.

"Helen Keller is a wreck!" one paper reported.

"The young girl is dwelling constantly on the thought of death!" reported another.

Annie ignored these stories, thankful that Helen was back home away from the negative forces of her ever-increasing fame. Although Helen was far from suicidal, Annie was worried about her. Helen was reluctant even to read now, fearing that somehow she'd accidentally "steal" what she read. Helen would go for hours without writing in Annie's hand or trying to talk. Annie knew she had to do something.

"Why don't you write about your own life?" Annie asked her one morning. "So many people would be interested in what you have to say and what it's like to be you."

Helen wasn't sure.

"How can I be sure the ideas are my own?" she wrote slowly in Annie's hand.

Annie explained that if Helen was writing about herself and how she felt, it would have to be original. No one else could have ever written what was in Helen's heart.

Helen was not convinced, but slowly and somewhat fearfully, she began to write a story about herself. She described what it was like to be both deaf and blind, and how it felt to live in a world of people who could see and hear. She wrote about being a child whose life did not really begin until she was eight years old. The story was wonderful—so wonderful that it was published in a magazine for children. This time, no one wrote any angry letters. Instead, letters of praise, love, and admiration poured in from all over the country. Both children and adults told Helen that her writing was inspiring and so very interesting. It made them want to meet her and be her friend.

Helen's smile returned as Annie read the letters to her. The nightmare of "The Frost King" was finally over. Helen was ready to move on.

In the spring and summer of 1893, Helen and Annie did some traveling with Alexander Graham Bell. Because of Bell's fame and now Helen's, crowds of people often followed them around. As Helen, Annie, and Bell picnicked at Niagara Falls, photographers hurried to get pictures. Other visitors to the falls were more interested in staring at Helen than at the magnificent rushing water. More than anything, people were curious about how Helen could enjoy Niagara if she could neither see nor hear the falls.

"I felt the air vibrate and the earth tremble," Helen explained. "It seems strange to many people that I should be impressed by the wonders and beauties of Niagara. They are always asking: 'What does this beauty or that music mean to you? You cannot see the waves rolling up the beach or hear their roar. What can they mean to you?' In the most evident sense, they mean everything."

Helen walked fearlessly across a shaking and trembling suspension bridge stretched across the falls. The sensation of all that roaring power surrounding her thrilled Helen. Bell suggested that Helen hug a pillow against her chest as she walked across the bridge.

"But why?" Helen wrote into Bell's hand.

"You'll see," Bell replied.

Much to Helen's surprise and amazement, the pillow acted as something of a vibrations conductor. She could feel Niagara Falls right to the center of her being.

Later that summer, Helen, Annie, and Bell went to the World's Fair in Chicago. The World's Fair was a huge event that went on for half a year. The fairgrounds took up nearly 700 acres, and 27 million people came from all over the world to see the wonders at the fair. The fair was a celebration of the 400th anniversary of Columbus's arrival in America, complete with life-sized replicas of Columbus's three ships. But the fair also included replicas of wonders from every corner of the world. And Helen was allowed to touch all of them. She spent three weeks at the fair, touching Egyptian pyramids, a model of Cairo, a Viking ship, ancient stone tools, and even mummies. One afternoon, Helen and Annie took a ride high up in the air on a brand-new invention by a man named George Ferris: the Ferris wheel.

"Every day in imagination, I made a trip around the world," Helen wrote. "I saw many marvels of invention. . . . All the activities of human life actually passed under my fingertips."

By the end of the summer, Helen felt differently about herself and the world around her. Now a teenager, she had moved on from fairytales and dolls. She had come to realize just how much the world had to offer. And perhaps more importantly, she was now beginning to think about how much she might be able to offer back to this wonderful world.

Chapter 7

"Look! Look! It's Helen Keller and Annie Sullivan!"

A small crowd gathered along the horse path in Central Park to watch the two riders go by. Now at Wright-Humason School for the Deaf in New York City, Helen rode her horse nearly every afternoon in the park. Annie had to lead the way, of course, and set the pace on her horse. However, Helen had become such a good and even daring rider that Annie often let the horses gallop swiftly through the park. As the gawking crowd grew, Annie frowned.

"Let's go!" she said to her horse and shook the reins. Behind her, Helen's horse sped up gradually as Helen laughed her loud, awkward laugh. Some of the boys in the crowd tried to run alongside the horses, but they were soon left behind. Annie sighed and shook her head as the horses slowed to a trot near a rose garden. Helen seemed to honestly enjoy her growing number of fans, but all the attention bothered Annie.

"Much has been said and written about Helen

Keller," Annie wrote to a friend. "Too much, I think, has appeared in type. One can scarcely take up a newspaper or magazine without finding an exaggerated account of her so-called 'marvelous accomplishments.'"

Annie continued to believe that the only "marvelous" thing about Helen was that she could read and write somewhat better than the average hearing and seeing child. Helen was simply a very bright girl who was receiving incredible opportunities and making the most of them. Annie knew something about beating the odds and receiving opportunities. And though she'd certainly not been a famous child, she knew that too much distraction and too much fame could hurt Helen's chances of living a happy, normal life. As a result, Annie was very protective of Helen for the two years Helen attended school in New York City.

At her new school, Helen continued studying math, literature and history. And because she was now in a school for the deaf, there were more teachers who could help Helen speak more clearly. Although long sentences were still hard for Helen to manage, she could often make herself understood when she spoke short phrases. Usually, Annie would spell into Helen's hand what was being spoken in a room where conversation was taking place. But sometimes Annie would become so involved in conversation that she would forget to write in Helen's hand. In the past, Helen would tug at Annie's arm. Now she would simply demand, in her loud and jarring voice, "WHAT'S GOING ON?"

Although Helen's speaking voice did not improve much during her time in New York, she did learn a new valuable skill. Helen discovered that at her new school, deaf students often learned how to "read lips." This meant they could learn, over time, what words were being formed simply by watching a person's mouth move. This was, of course, faster and easier for communication than sign language.

Could I learn to read lips by touching them when someone is speaking? Helen wondered. Although this method of communication was very unusual and rarely taught, it was indeed possible. Helen practiced by touching Annie's lips as Annie formed words. As with nearly everything Helen attempted, this was very difficult at first. But in time, Helen caught on. Soon, she was able to "hear" Annie speaking through touch. Now, when Alexander Graham Bell came to New York for a visit, Helen was able to communicate with Annie and Bell at the same time! Graham spelled into Helen's right hand while her left hand read Annie's lips.

During her time in New York City, many rich and famous people invited Helen to parties, dinners, and events. At one such event, fourteen-year-old Helen met the famous author Mark Twain. Twain was not one to be impressed by well-known people, but Helen was an exception. He was astonished when this deaf and blind girl was able to discuss many of his books and ask thoughtful questions about the characters in her awkward speaking voice. Annie spelled Twain's words into Helen's hand.

"Then I told her a story which she interrupted all along and in the right places, with cackles, chuckles, and carefree bursts of laughter," Twain later wrote. "A wonderful child . . ."

Helen gently touched Twain's face and wild, messy hair to get an idea of his appearance. She grinned and touched his face again. She then kissed Twain on the cheek and put a violet in the buttonhole of his coat before leaving. Twain would never forget it.

But as much as Helen loved meeting people, how much wealth or power someone had meant nothing to her. One evening, she and Annie were guests of the "Millionaires' Club." Nearly everyone at the dinner was fabulously rich, and the surroundings at the famous Metropolitan Club building were very fancy and expensive. Helen was polite, but she did not particularly enjoy her time among the millionaires.

"The building is magnificent, being built of white marble," she wrote after that evening. "The rooms are large and splendidly furnished; but I must confess, so much splendor is rather oppressive to me. . . . I didn't envy the millionaires in the least all the happiness their gorgeous surroundings are supposed to bring them."

Still, Helen enjoyed (and would continue to enjoy) many advantages, thanks to the contributions that rich people made toward her education and lifestyle. Although the Kellers were by no means poor, they would not have been able to afford to send Helen to a special school in New York City. Helen dressed and ate well. She took cruises on luxurious sailboats up the Hudson River and enjoyed a guided visit to the Statue of Liberty. And, of course, she always had her teacher at her side. Helen knew she was lucky and had advantages that others did not have. But one Saturday morning, Helen would realize just how lucky she was.

"Let's go to a different part of the city today," Annie said to Helen. Helen, always up for a new adventure, quickly agreed. The two of them took a streetcar to an area of the city known as the Lower East Side. Immediately, Helen could sense that things were very different in this part of the city. Helen stood still and turned around. She smelled the air.

"Where are we?" she asked Annie.

"In the tenement slums," Annie wrote back. "Where poor people live."

From 1800 to 1880, the population of New York City had doubled every decade as new immigrants poured in, mostly from Europe. Many of these new immigrants lived in the Lower East

Side, where housing was cheapest. But as the population grew, landlords divided up apartments, making them smaller and smaller. And as more people arrived in New York and jobs became scarcer, people became poorer and had even less money to spend on rent. As a result, these tiny one-room "tenements" (a word for a rented living space) often had eight to ten people living in them.

Crowded living conditions were not the worst of it. Many tenements were dangerously old and filthy, were filled with rats, and lacked plumbing and electricity. Illness often swept through the Lower East Side. Only a few decades before Helen was born, 5,000 people living in these New York City slums died of an illness called cholera. Children who had been abandoned by parents lived in the streets and slept in doorways. Hardly anyone had enough to eat.

Now, as Helen and Annie slowly walked along Mulberry Street, Helen sensed how different life was here. She couldn't see the poverty surrounding her, but she could smell it—the filth, the sickness, and even the rats. Heavy smoke drifted up from burning trash. People without kitchens cooked cheap food over small fires along the sidewalks. Sweating horses, garbage, mud and dust—all these smells painted a vivid mental picture for Helen.

And Helen's fingertips felt this strange new place, too. There were the crumbling brick walls of the tenements. A dog that padded alongside Helen had a thin and mangy coat. Apples on a cart were small, and the cart itself was smooth and fragile with age. Paint and rust peeled from lampposts. And as strangers passed by on the overcrowded street, Helen's hands brushed against the rough, cheap material of their clothing. At one point, Helen could smell the damp and moldy scent of an alleyway. She felt a strange rumbling as they passed it and reached for Annie's arm.

"Children playing with empty barrels," Annie explained.

"Barrels?" Helen asked, cocking her head to one side in confusion. She'd never heard of that.

"They don't have toys," Annie explained. "So they roll barrels in the alley for fun."

Helen walked along quietly, holding Annie's hand. She certainly knew there were people less fortunate than herself in the world, but she'd never been surrounded by them before. In ways those who can hear and see cannot understand, she could *feel* a sorrow and a heaviness all around her. She thought of the rich people in their fancy homes with plenty to eat. The millionaires were a small and exclusive club, but these poor people flooded the streets. The crumbling tenements went on and on for many blocks—much farther than Helen and Annie could walk that afternoon.

It isn't fair, Helen thought to herself.

As she walked on through the slums, tears sprang to her eyes, and a fire was lit inside of her.

Helen was not sure what she could do or how she would do it, but from that point on, she became determined to aid the poor and the powerless. It had not been that long ago that Helen had been utterly powerless herself—until someone came along to help her. Helen hugged Annie's arm and made a silent vow to help others.

"My own dear father!" Helen wrote in a letter to a friend when she was sixteen. "How shall I ever bear it!"

Captain Keller had died suddenly during Helen's second year at school in New York. Naturally, Helen was upset to lose her father, but her grief was made worse when her mother would not allow her to travel to Alabama for the funeral. Mrs. Keller claimed that the stress and hot weather would make Helen sick, but Helen knew that was not the real reason why her mother told her and Annie not to come. Did her mother feel awkward around her now? Helen wasn't sure. She and her mother had grown apart gradually over the years. During that time, Annie had become more like a mother to Helen. They were always together. Helen depended upon Annie completely and rarely needed her mother anymore. Perhaps during this time of great sorrow, Mrs. Keller could not bear to deal with the added feelings of loss when it came to Helen.

Helen had learned a great deal about religion, and she spent many hours thinking about it. Her own faith in God had become strong. It was this faith that helped her deal with the death of her father.

"I forgot my heartache, and only thought of my dear father in his heavenly home, surrounded by angels and learning all he could not learn here," Helen later wrote not long after her father died. "What a great comfort those truths are to me. Oh, I have never needed them so sorely before."

Making something of her life and learning as much as she could during her time on earth became even more important to Helen after the death of Captain Keller. She was growing restless at the Wright-Humason School. In many ways, she and Annie both felt that she had learned all she could learn there. And some of the teachers suggested that, at sixteen, Helen did not need further education. But Helen disagreed.

"I want to go to college," she told Annie one morning.

Annie discouraged Helen. It was rare for women to go to college in the 1890s. Those who did go to college often attended for only one or two years, until they married. Certainly, it was not unheard of for women to obtain college degrees. But college-educated women were often looked at as being different or strange. Many men were not interested in a woman with a lot of education. In addition, no deaf and blind person had ever gone to college.

None of this mattered to Helen.

"I want to go to Harvard," she added, disregarding Annie's warnings.

In spite of herself, Annie had to smile. Not only had Helen chosen the most difficult school to get into in the country; she had chosen a college that, at the time, accepted only male students.

"Harvard is a men's school," Annie explained. "Radcliffe College is Harvard's sister school for women."

Without a second thought, Helen replied, "Then I will go to Radcliffe."

But it wasn't as simple as Helen deciding to go to Radcliffe. She had to be accepted there first. And it was exceedingly difficult to get accepted. In order to prepare for the Radcliffe entrance exams, Helen and Annie decided that Helen should continue her studies at the Cambridge School for Young Ladies. This school, located near Radcliffe, was specifically designed for preparing young women for the Radcliffe entrance exams.

The director of the school, Arthur Gilman, was impressed with Helen's fame and determination, but he wasn't so sure about Annie Sullivan. Gilman had heard ugly rumors about her. Some people said that Annie helped Helen cheat on tests and that she was simply using Helen to make money. Gilman, unfortunately, believed these rumors and, as a result, watched Annie closely. He refused to let her be in the same room with Helen when she took tests. He disregarded Annie's opinions. Furthermore, Gilman knew that Annie's parents had been poor Irish immigrants. Shouldn't Helen, who came from a much better background, have a "better" teacher?

Meanwhile, Annie continued to push Helen to be the best she could be. She demanded near-perfection from her student. Sometimes Annie's naturally fiery personality made her frustrated or short-tempered with Helen when Helen had difficulty understanding something. But Helen accepted all of this as part of the learning process. She knew Teacher wanted only the best for her, and she loved Teacher for that.

"You push her too hard," Gilman said to Annie.

"I do not!" Annie replied angrily. "And I don't need your advice for *my* student."

Gilman would not stand for a woman, particularly one of a lower class, to speak to him in this way. Bit by bit, he became convinced that Annie was bad for Helen. Then, during her second year at the school, Helen became sick for a few days. The sickness was mild, but Gilman told other teachers that he was sure that Annie was driving Helen to a nervous breakdown. He made a decision.

"We must not blind ourselves to the truth," Gilman wrote in a letter to Mrs. Keller. "The time has come for Miss Sullivan to leave Helen."

Chapter 8

Back in Alabama, Mrs. Keller read Gilman's letter in shock.

"Helen is being pushed to exhaustion by Miss Sullivan."

"Miss Sullivan does not care about Helen."

"Miss Sullivan is not smart enough for Helen."

"Helen deserves a teacher from a better background."

Mrs. Keller reread the letter twice and thought about it. She had long watched Annie demand a lot from Helen. She hadn't ever been worried, but maybe she should have been! Could it be true that Annie was merely using Helen to make money?

Finally, after much thought, she wrote back to Mr. Gilman.

"I thank you for your timely warning on Helen's behalf. I hope I have too much sense to allow a daughter to be taxed beyond her strength. . . . An immediate change must be made."

The immediate change that Gilman suggested was to make *him* Helen's legal guardian—not Annie. Believing she was acting in Helen's best interests, Mrs. Keller wrote back: "You are authorized to act as Helen's guardian."

Gilman was thrilled.

He was far less concerned about Helen's well-being than he was about being the guardian of the world-famous Helen Keller. Think of what this might do for his school! In contrast to Annie's feelings about Helen's fame, Gilman could not wait to use Helen to promote the reputation of the Cambridge School. His plan seemed to be succeeding until . . .

"If Helen and I are separated, it will be at the cost of two dead bodies!" Annie shouted dramatically at Gilman when he told her that she was no longer needed. "I'm leaving with her immediately."

"But you can't," Gilman said with a smug grin. "You are no longer her guardian."

Annie felt as though the wind had been knocked out of her. With angry tears streaming down her face, she returned to Helen, determined to finish Helen's Greek lesson before telling her what was going on. But Helen felt her teacher's hands shaking.

"I was utterly bewildered," Helen later wrote. "She told me about a letter to my mother from someone who expressed his opinion that Miss

Sullivan and I should be separated! Mr. Gilman, whom I had trusted, had done it all."

When Annie left a few days later, Helen clung to her and sobbed all the way out the door. What would she do without Teacher? Everything she knew, everything she had learned, even her ability to understand love and God had been thanks to Annie's hard work. This wasn't right!

Now Helen became truly ill. She neither slept nor ate. She sat in corners weeping and holding her head in her hands.

Annie was not much better. On her way out of Cambridge, she stood on a bridge and looked down at the cold Charles River and thought about drowning herself. But Annie's determination was stronger than her sorrow. She wrote to Mrs. Keller and pleaded with her, letting her know that she and Helen needed to be together. She then contacted Alexander Graham Bell and other friends who believed in her, asking them to also write to Mrs. Keller. Finally, a confused Mrs. Keller came to Cambridge. When she saw the state her daughter was in, Mrs. Keller was furious. She withdrew Helen from Gilman's school, canceled his guardian status, and returned Helen to Annie.

"I had never doubted Teacher," Helen later expressed. "We were closer than ever."

During that time, Helen also admitted to Annie that if her mother had not changed her mind, and Helen had had to choose between her mother and her teacher, she would have chosen Annie.

"We will be together always," she promised Teacher.

Helen continued preparing for the Radcliffe entrance exams with the help of a private tutor. For another year and a half, she studied Greek, Latin, literature, geometry and algebra. Languages and literature were easy for Helen, but math remained a terrible struggle. Making matters worse, when the exams came around, the math tests were written in a type of Braille that Helen could not read well. Radcliffe would not allow Annie to be with Helen during the exams, and they refused to change the type of Braille.

Nonetheless, Helen passed the exams. She was ready to go to Radcliffe! However, Radcliffe was not ready for Helen. The president of the college now claimed that Helen would never be able to keep up with the other students. Annie was furious. She believed Mr. Gilman, who was close friends with the president, was creating all these problems for Helen out of spite. Annie begged Helen to go to a different school. She had already been fully accepted at a number of excellent colleges. But Helen refused.

Later, Helen admitted with a sheepish smile, "I insisted on going to Radcliffe because they didn't want me."

Helen wrote a long letter to Radcliffe's president, describing how hard she had worked and how much she wanted to attend his wonderful college.

"You must let me *try*," Helen wrote. "A true soldier does not admit defeat before battle."

Helen's letter must have impressed the president. In the fall of 1900, Helen Keller became the first deaf and blind person to go to college.

Helen's years at Radcliffe were very hard. While other students could take notes during classes, Helen had to remember everything Annie wrote in her hand. Often, she would rush back to her room and use an unusual typewriter that typed in Braille to write down what she could remember. The college watched Annie suspiciously. Many people could not believe that a blind and deaf girl could make it through college.

"When people found out that Helen was to enter Radcliffe, there was a lot of talk," one teacher recalled. "Everyone thought it was Miss Sullivan, not Helen, who would do all the work."

As a result, Annie was not allowed to help Helen beyond the classroom other than reading books to Helen that were not in Braille. And she was certainly not allowed to be with Helen during tests. Helen found that she had to work nearly twice as hard as students who could see and hear. She often spent fifteen or more hours a day getting all her work done. She missed the days of discussing poetry and ideas with Teacher, the mornings of walking and discovering.

"One goes to college to learn, it seems, not to think," Helen wrote during that time.

And beyond schoolwork, things were also difficult for Helen. The other girls at the college did not quite know what to do about Helen. They certainly did not know how to communicate with her. So, mostly, they ignored her. On occasion, girls might shake Helen's hand, but even then, Helen felt a distance, a kind of odd worry in the touch of their hands.

"Some hands, when they clasp yours, bubble over with gladness," Helen wrote. "Other people shake hands with me as if with the fear that I may do them mischief."

This was a lonely time for Helen. She and Annie lived in a small apartment off campus, and there was rarely any free time to visit old friends or meet new people. Even Helen's teachers seemed to keep their distance from her. Helen often felt that they didn't want her in their classes. The one exception was Helen's English teacher, Dr. Copeland. He was warm and encouraging, and he took special interest in Helen.

"Her writing is among the best I have ever seen in my classes," he told Annie. He felt that Helen should stop trying to write like all the other girls. Helen wrote about enjoying a spring day, for example, the way any young person might. But certainly, Dr. Copeland explained, her ways of experiencing that day would be much different.

"Why don't you write stories about yourself?" Dr. Copeland asked Helen. "Write from *your* experience."

As always, Helen could not really understand why others would be interested in her life. Why would anyone want to read that kind of "story"? But her English teacher convinced her that many people would, indeed, love to read that story.

"I have always accepted other people's experiences. . . . It never occurred to me that it might be worthwhile to describe the experiences that are peculiarly my own," she wrote to Dr. Copeland. "From now on, I am resolved to be myself, to live my own life, and write my own thoughts when I have any. . . ."

And although Helen was not convinced that she would have thoughts that would interest others, she certainly did. What she began writing attracted the attention of the editors of a national magazine. The magazine asked Helen to write a series of stories over the course of several months, and they offered her $3000! In 1901, the average *yearly* salary in the United States was about $700, so this was a huge amount of money.

Although several wealthy people continued to help pay for Helen's education, she never had quite enough money. And it often made both Helen and Annie uncomfortable to accept donations, so they frequently turned down money. Helen later explained that she was flattered to have her "little stories" published, but being able to earn her own money made her feel even better. Plenty of people, even those who were fans of Helen's, did not believe that a blind and deaf person could actually "do" anything to earn a living. Helen was determined to prove these people wrong.

However, it was nearly impossible for Helen to keep up with her classes and write her stories too. Sometimes, the magazine demanded a story before Helen had had a chance to make corrections and edit what she had written. She couldn't bear the thought of turning in poor work to the magazine. Finally, a friend introduced Helen and Annie to a 25-year-old English teacher at Harvard, John Macy. John was a very good writer and an even better editor. He agreed to help Helen with her stories, doing editing and organizing. John was so impressed with Helen's writing that he suggested she put all the stories together into a book.

Helen agreed, and before she was even 23 years old, she had published her first book, titled *The Story of My Life*. Although, the book did not sell many copies right away, it eventually sold many hundreds of thousands of copies and became an American classic. In 1996, it was named one of the most important books of the century!

John Macy was not impressed only by Helen—he equally admired Annie Sullivan. He found it hard to understand why many people seemed to dislike Annie. Because Annie did not like to draw attention to herself, some people believed she was either hiding something or was unfriendly. John Macy did not see her that way.

"I must say a word about the good and sweet woman who has been with Miss Keller for 15 years. . . . Independent and willful as her pupil, Miss Sullivan has shut the door against the world and says, 'It is nobody's business who I am; I want Helen to stand on her own feet.'"

To John, Annie's fiery personality, her stubbornness, and her quiet support of Helen made her more, not less, likable. In fact, it made her so likeable that John found himself falling in love with Annie. Annie felt the same way about John, but when he asked her to marry him, she was reluctant to say yes.

"What will Helen think?" Annie wondered.

"Why don't we ask her?" John replied.

But Annie didn't want her love life to interfere with Helen's studies, so for another year and a half, she refused to marry John or talk about it with Helen.

Finally, in June of 1904, Helen graduated from Radcliffe. It had been a long and hard journey, but Helen graduated *cum laude*, meaning "with praise." A degree with honors was difficult to earn at Radcliffe, but Helen had done it. When she and Annie walked across the stage to receive her diploma, the crowd stood to cheer and give Helen a standing ovation. Helen thought Annie should receive a diploma too. After all, Annie had read to Helen until her eyes almost failed again, attended classes with Helen, and helped her prepare for exams. Surely she was deserving of equal praise and reward. Why did so many people ignore her hard work?

Helen was somewhat bitter about how Teacher was treated. But Annie was not. As she watched Helen grasp the diploma and smile, Annie thought of how far the little girl who threw plates and locked people in pantries had come. In 17 years, Helen Keller had gone from being "a phantom living in a no-world" to being the only deaf and blind college graduate that the world had ever seen. Annie looked at her student proudly and clapped as loudly as anyone in the audience.

Only days after graduation, John Macy asked Helen what she would think about Annie marrying him. Helen wanted Teacher to be happy, so she told John that she would be glad for the two of them to be married. Annie assured Helen that she would still be at her side at all times. Indeed, Helen would live with John and Annie in John's old farmhouse in Massachusetts. If Helen felt awkward about the living situation, she never expressed her feelings. But certainly,

Annie's marriage made her think about her own feelings toward love and marriage.

Helen was a young and beautiful woman. She was tall, with long chestnut hair and a wide, appealing smile. And though one of her eyes was slightly deformed, many thought her eyes were particularly sweet. In addition to her looks, Helen was bright, funny, and kind. Although the young women at Radcliffe had never been particularly friendly to Helen, the young men Helen met at the many dinners and gatherings that she and Annie attended often showed interest in her. Some gazed at her shyly, unsure of how to approach her. Others engaged in conversation with Helen through Annie for as long as Annie would allow it. More than one young man expressed a desire to see Helen again.

Helen was always polite to her admirers. But was she interested in romance, too?

"Helen, a day must come when love, which is more than friendship, will knock at the door of your heart and demand to be let in," Alexander Graham Bell once said to Helen. He had noticed that though Helen had many young men paying attention to her, she never became anything more than a friend to them.

"I do think about love sometimes," Helen admitted quietly. "But it is like a beautiful flower which I may not touch."

Bell was troubled by this answer. "Do you think that because you cannot see or hear, you are not allowed to have the same kind of happiness that other women have?"

"Oh, but I am very happy," Helen replied. "I have my teacher and all kinds of interesting things to do. I don't care a bit about being married."

"Are you sure?" Graham asked doubtfully.

"I can't imagine a man wanting to marry me," Helen finally said. "I should think it would seem like marrying a statue."

Helen tried hard to convince her old friend Alexander Graham Bell, but Bell had known Helen for many years now. He could read her expression with his eyes and know what was in her heart the same way Helen could hold her old friend's hand and know if he was troubled. And now as Graham gazed at Helen, he could clearly see a glimmer of sadness.

Chapter 9

"**I** suppose you will smile when I say that I especially enjoy canoeing on moonlight nights," Helen wrote in *The Story of My Life*. "I cannot, it is true, see the moon climb up in the sky behind the pines, but I know she is there, and as I lie back and put my hand in the water, I believe I can feel the shimmer of her garments as she passes."

It was writing like this that made so many people curious about Helen Keller. How could she *feel* the moon? And if she could feel it, how could she stand living in total darkness?

"It isn't really a black darkness," Helen explained. "It's a white darkness." Helen described it as a foggy gray. Furthermore, Helen described the wonder of her dreams at night in which she "heard the trampling of many waters" and often saw a bright light. Once she saw a sparkling pearl resting in her own hands. From coast to coast, people were amazed. They wanted to meet Helen, see her, hear her speak. There was suddenly a public demand for Helen to go on a speaking tour. It could mean a lot of money for

Helen, and now that she was finished with college, she needed an income. John did not earn enough to support all three of them, and Helen didn't expect to be supported by Annie's husband.

But as was often the case, there were far more important things to Helen than money.

During the long evenings at John's farmhouse, the talk often turned to politics. John Macy, along with a number of Americans at that time, was a socialist. Most Americans still believed in capitalism. In capitalism, the American form of economics, people and companies own property and businesses without the government interfering. Capitalism encourages competition in business. As a result, a business that competes well makes a lot of money. And some business owners become very rich. At the same time, however, many more people (most often employees of the businesses) remain poor.

Socialism, on the other hand, discourages a system in which very rich people control most of the money and property. Socialists feel that businesses and property should be owned by society as a whole. Everything is shared mostly equally so that there is no "wealth inequality"—a situation that occurs when a small number of people have the most money. When wealth is so unequally divided, the middle class shrinks. And when that happens, more and more people become poor.

Helen listened and thought about all of this with interest. She recalled her walk through New York's

Lower East Side years earlier. John explained that many of the people there were terribly poor due to wealth inequality. They struggled at jobs in factories and businesses owned by very wealthy people who paid them next to nothing. Helen cringed when she thought about how she had eaten dinner with some of the very millionaires who might be making the lives of these people miserable. Worst of all, to Helen, was the fact that blindness was so common among these poor people as a result of disease, poor nutrition, and lack of funds for medical care.

"And often it could be prevented by a simple and cheap treatment," John explained.

"But that's terrible!" Helen said. "Why doesn't the government do something about it?"

John didn't have an easy answer. It seemed that the government was typically more likely to pay attention to the rich than to the poor. Helen was outraged. What poor people faced reminded her of the life she had lived before Teacher came along—trapped, sad, and desperate. In response to her anger, Helen did what she did best: she wrote. In an article for a national magazine, she talked about an eye infection that babies got if their mothers had a sexually transmitted disease known as syphilis. The infection almost always led to blindness, but it could be prevented by putting a few simple drops of cheap medicine into the infants' eyes.

Many readers were surprised by Helen's article. In those days, women didn't write about sexually transmitted diseases, poverty, and injustice. But Helen did.

And that was just the beginning. Over the next several years, Helen devoted herself to bringing more awareness to the problems of the blind, poor people, and women.

"The few own the many," Helen wrote in an angry article about the mistreatment of the poor. "The country is governed for the richest, for the corporations, the bankers. . . . The majority of mankind are working people. . . . The majority of mankind is ground down by industrial oppression in order that the small remnant may live in ease."

In addition, Helen was outraged that women were not allowed to vote. She marched in protests with suffragists—women who were demanding that right. At the time, the suffragists were often viewed as being outspoken, radical, and even crazy. Some people couldn't imagine why Helen Keller, of all people, was involved with them. Did she even understand what she was doing? Helen certainly did. In an even bolder and more unusual move, Helen wrote an article in which she supported birth control for women. Some people were shocked that Helen would even mention birth control, much less openly support the use of it.

As the public became more uneasy with Helen, she kept right on working and marching and writing. In 1913, she published a book titled *Out of the Dark*. In this little book, she wrote about why she was a socialist and why she believed socialism was important for the United States. The book sold barely any copies. In addition, many people became angry with Helen. Some felt that socialism was wrong and that those who supported it were anti-American.

And some people were simply upset that Helen had changed. *What happened to the sweet little girl we all knew?* many people wondered. They wanted to see the helpless blind and deaf girl who had posed for pictures on horseback or at Niagara Falls. They wanted to hear her struggling to speak and recite pleasant poetry and Bible verses. Who *was* this angry young woman with a mind of her own? How dare she have opinions!

One angry newspaper columnist who had praised and admired the "miraculous" teenaged Helen in his paper, the *Brooklyn Eagle*, now changed his mind about her. After reading about Helen's support of socialism and women's right to vote, the columnist wrote that Helen, apparently, was not the person he thought she was. Further, he claimed that Helen's "mistakes" were a result of her blindness and deafness. He implied that Helen was stupid due to her inability to see or hear.

"At that time the compliments he paid me were so generous that I blush to remember them!" a furious Helen fired back. "But now that I have come out for socialism, he reminds me and the public that I am blind and deaf and especially liable to error. I must have shrunk in intelligence during the years since I met him. . . . Oh, ridiculous *Brooklyn Eagle!* Socially blind and deaf, it defends an intolerable system, a system that is the cause of much of the physical blindness and deafness which we are trying to prevent!"

Helen was puzzled by the public's reaction. She thought it only natural that an educated woman with a mind of her own should express her ideas and beliefs. Unfortunately, many people of that era believed just the opposite. Most men, and many women, believed a woman should be quiet and sweet and keep her opinions to herself.

By 1914, Helen finally decided to go on the speaking tour that she had been putting off. Annie and John were beginning to argue more and more often. Helen knew that part of the problem was a lack of money. Although many people did not understand this "new" adult Helen, they were still very curious about her, and Helen knew they would buy tickets to her shows. Annie and Helen planned the show together. Annie would begin by talking about her work with Helen when Helen was a girl. Then Helen would come onstage and talk about herself, both through Annie and through speaking herself.

For several months, Helen worked hard on her speaking voice, but she knew it was not very good. Because of this, Helen experienced terrible stage fright at first.

"My mind froze, my heart stopped beating," Helen wrote about her first show. "Until my dying day, I shall think of that stage as a pillory [a whipping post] where I stood cold, trembling, voiceless."

In spite of this shaky beginning, Helen's show, titled *The Heart and the Hand*, was a hit. People jammed theaters all over the country to see Helen and Annie. At the end of the show, Helen always took questions from the audience. It was her favorite part of the show, and she always tried to answer the questions with honesty or good-natured humor:

"Do you close your eyes to sleep?"

"I guess I do, but I never stayed awake to find out."

"Can you enjoy trees?"

"Yes, they speak to me of the silent works of God."

"What do you think of the Ku Klux Klan?"

"I like them about as much as I do a hornet's nest."

"Who are your best friends?"

"Books."

The Heart and the Hand continued along successfully, but Annie was feeling overwhelmed. Although Helen had come to love performing, Annie found it exhausting and stressful. Between the work of touring, performing, and looking after Helen, Annie often became depressed or ill. Helen and Annie decided to hire an assistant. His name was Peter Fagan. Peter was young, handsome, and full of jokes and stories. Helen liked Peter right away, but Peter developed even stronger feelings for Helen. One evening, when Helen was alone, Peter took her hand gently and spelled his feelings into her palm.

"I was surprised that he cared so much about me," Helen later wrote. "There was sweet comfort in his loving words. I listened all a-tremble."

Soon, Peter and Helen were together all the time, taking walks in the woods, talking until late in the night, sharing dreams and plans.

"His love was a bright sun that shone upon me," Helen wrote. "The sweetness of being loved enchanted me."

Peter asked Helen to marry him, and Helen happily said yes. Almost immediately, they applied for a marriage license in Boston amid a flurry of reporters and photographers who couldn't wait to be the first to report that Helen Keller was getting married. But when Helen's mother found out through a newspaper story—Helen had been afraid to tell her—she was furious. Although Helen was in her late thirties, Mrs. Keller still thought of her as a young girl. She felt that Peter was only trying to control her "helpless" deaf and blind daughter. Mrs. Keller refused to give Helen her blessing to get married.

Helen and Peter realized that their only choice was to elope. But somehow Mrs. Keller found out about their plans and wrote to Peter. She angrily told him to stay away from Helen. Helen, believing that their elopement was still on, waited an entire night on the front porch with a packed suitcase. But Peter never showed up. And Helen never heard from him again.

Rather than feeling sorry for herself and being angry at her mother, Helen blamed herself for doing something she later claimed was foolish.

"I cannot account for my behavior," Helen wrote. "I seem to have acted exactly opposite to my nature."

Still, Helen's "nature" always leaned toward love, and there is no doubt that she was in love with Peter.

"The brief love will remain in my life, a little island of joy surrounded by dark waters," Helen remembered in a bittersweet letter to a friend. "The fault was not in the loving, but in the circumstances."

In 1917, the United States entered World War I. Both Annie and Helen opposed the war, and they were not shy about speaking out about it. Soon, however, they found that people were not eager to part with their money to listen to two socialist women who were openly anti-war. Furthermore, the United States government looked suspiciously at anyone who publicly disagreed with the war effort. Doing so could lead to arrest and even imprisonment. Helen and Annie agreed to take a break.

Although Helen was as eager as ever for new adventures as soon as possible, Annie was not. She had been very sick for much of the past year, and now she and John had separated and were on unfriendly terms. John blamed Annie for being gone too much and for spending too much time with Helen. When Annie refused to divorce John, he moved to New York and became involved with another woman. Annie was heartbroken, angry, and depressed. Helen worried about Teacher and did whatever she could to assure Annie that things would be all right. But as the money from their shows began to dwindle, Helen found it harder and harder to believe her own words. Before long, the two women were forced to move into a small apartment. They were counting their pennies and living on cheap food. Annie's health never seemed to get much better, and now her eyes were bothering her again.

What to do? What to do? Helen wondered anxiously as she paced the small kitchen of the apartment. As Annie got older, Helen felt responsible for Teacher. Teacher had opened the world to Helen more than three decades earlier and had faithfully remained by Helen's side. Helen often referred to March 3, 1887 as her "soul's birthday," because that was the day Annie arrived in Alabama. It was the beginning of Helen's discovery of her own soul. In many ways, it was more important to Helen than her real birthday. Helen knew she owed it to Teacher to take care of her. But how?

Strong in faith, Helen prayed for some kind of answer, some kind of help. And then, in the spring of 1918, it arrived. Out of the blue, Hollywood came calling.

Chapter 10

"**A** movie about you would be wonderful!" a Hollywood movie producer said excitedly to Helen. "If you can find joy and light in everyday things, yours is the story people need to see right now."

As World War I raged on, many Americans looked for anything to take their minds off all the sorrow and death. One of the main forms of entertainment that many turned to was "moving pictures," or movies, as they would later be called. Movies were still a fairly new thing, and in 1918, movies were still silent. But people were astonished to watch pictures that actually moved on a screen. It seemed like magic!

In her typical fashion, Helen was eager to try this new experience. Not only did she assume that it would provide an income for her and Annie; she also believed that her story would inspire and help people.

"It will help me carry farther the message that has so long burned in my heart," Helen explained. "A message of courage, a message of a brighter, happier future for all. . . . I desire to open wide all the prison-doors of the world."

Annie, who was also to appear in the movie, was not so sure. She thought Helen's imagination was working overtime if she really assumed a Hollywood movie was going to open "the prison-doors of the world." Annie was not impressed with the stars of Hollywood at the time, and she thought many movies were silly or overdone. Still, Annie saw it as a good opportunity for people to come to know Helen's amazing story, so she agreed to the movie.

Ready . . . Action!

In scene after scene, Helen was baffled. What in the world was going on? In one scene, the director asked her to sit down and type at her Braille typewriter. In another, she danced across a ballroom floor. In another, she was filmed taking off in an airplane. ("I felt rain clouds spilling their pearls upon me," Helen would later write.) In yet another, both Helen and Annie had to wear ridiculous costumes and go to a party where actors playing the parts of famous people, both living and dead, came over to talk to Helen. When Annie described the director's "vision" for the movie, Helen laughed out loud.

If Helen had hoped this movie would be her personal story of hope and courage, she was sadly mistaken. In reality, the movie was little more than a strange jumble of scenes showing the famous Helen Keller doing things most people would never expect a deaf and blind person to do. There was a vague message about hope overcoming sorrow, but it was by no means the "story" of Helen's life. Although Helen had fun in Hollywood and, as always, enjoyed meeting new people, she was disappointed.

"Will people even want to see this movie?" she asked Annie doubtfully.

Annie placed Helen's hand on her cheek and just shook her head.

Annie was right. The movie, *Deliverance* (so named because Helen was "delivered" from darkness), was a major flop. People were interested in Helen, but this movie was barely about her. Although *Deliverance* received some good reviews, mainly due to Helen's beauty and grace in front of the camera, it made hardly any money at all. Within a few months of returning to their apartment in New York, Helen and Annie were flat broke.

"How about trying out a vaudeville act?" a well-meaning friend asked Helen and Annie.

Annie gasped. "Absolutely not!"

"But vaudeville is even more popular than movies," the friend said. "You're sure to make a lot of money."

"We will not stoop that low," Annie replied icily.

"What's going on?" Helen asked loudly. She could tell by the way Teacher was moving that something was wrong, and Teacher had stopped writing in Helen's hand.

When Annie explained, Helen cocked her head to one side to think for several seconds. Then she smiled. Helen knew all about vaudeville. "Vaudeville" was the name given to shows that played all over the United States in small theaters, in bars, and even in circuses. A typical vaudeville show usually involved singing, juggling, performing animals, and comedy. However, some vaudeville shows presented what were known as "freak and odd acts." These included a man who swallowed frogs, an ex-convict who sang opera, two sisters who boxed each other, and a man with a singing duck.

Many upper-class people looked down on vaudeville shows. These shows typically attracted poorer people and factory workers. Audience members were encouraged to be rowdy, and many drank alcohol before and during the shows. Ticket prices were cheap because performers often did their shows multiple times a day. To many upper-class people, vaudeville performances were considered vulgar and not something decent people would waste their time with. This is how Annie felt, too.

It was not, however, how Helen felt.

"I found the world of vaudeville much more amusing than the world I had always lived in," Helen later recalled. "I liked to feel the warm tide of human life pulsing round and round me . . . the rush, glare, and noise of the life vibrations."

Although Helen had been disappointed with

Deliverance, she had truly enjoyed her experience in Hollywood. She loved being around the actors, the makeup, the costumes, and the warm lights. Perhaps vaudeville would not be as glamorous, but it sounded like fun to Helen. In addition, many vaudeville acts got paid very well. After days of arguing, begging, and reasoning, Helen finally convinced a very reluctant Annie to give vaudeville a try. In February, 1920, their show, *The Star of Happiness*, opened in New York City.

Helen was an instant hit on the vaudeville circuit. Many people who had been unable to afford tickets to her speaking tours now jammed theaters to see this "miracle" woman. In many ways, Helen was a national celebrity. Unlike other vaudeville acts, she didn't have to build up a name for herself and a following—she already had both. Helen's show was barely 20 minutes long, and parts of it were similar to the speaking tour show, with Annie speaking first and then Helen appearing. But there was also music, a voice offstage reciting dreamy poetry, and dramatic lighting.

"They're just coming to see if you will fall off the stage or make some other mistake," Annie said bitterly. She hated the entire vaudeville scene. Making things worse, Helen's show was only part of an entire evening of entertainment. Helen appeared right after stunt performers on stilts and just before a group of dancing women named "Luscious Looking Girls of Rare Joyousness and Bewitchment." Annie had been worried that Helen's show would fall into the "freak and odd acts" category, and it did.

But this did not mean that most people who saw Helen do her show thought she was a freak or odd. On the contrary, the many thousands of people from coast to coast who saw Helen in her vaudeville act were awed and inspired. If anyone had been expecting Helen to do "tricks" or make a fool of herself, they would have been disappointed.

"I who am blind can only give one hint to you who can see," Helen would say in her awkward voice near the end of the 20-minute show. A sudden hush would fall over the audience. "Use your eyes as if tomorrow you would go blind. Do the same with all your other senses. Hear the song of a bird as if tomorrow you would go deaf. Touch everything, smell the flowers, taste every bit of food as though you could no longer do any of these things tomorrow."

Often, audience members were moved to tears. Many people returned to see Helen again and again. And although Annie never enjoyed the years of vaudeville, she did enjoy the money it brought in. She and Helen were two of the highest-paid actors on in the country, often making up to $2,500 a week. That would be like earning nearly $30,000 a week today! Helen and Annie performed only a 20-minute show twice a day, but the job also required nearly nonstop traveling.

As an outspoken socialist, Helen sometimes felt guilty earning so much money, particularly when many of the audience members were poor. But in her heart, Helen believed she was doing the right thing. After World War I, so many people felt sad and hopeless. Seeing Helen often changed their outlook on life. In addition, Helen was happy to finally have money to take care of Teacher—and Annie needed more and more care. She was frequently sick, and her eyesight was getting dimmer. Then, one night, Annie collapsed onstage. A bad case of the flu combined with exhaustion put an end to Annie's vaudeville days.

Helen insisted that the show go on. Shows were still selling out across the country, and unlike Annie, Helen loved performing. But how would she do it without Teacher? Once again, Helen and Annie decided to find an assistant. Polly Thomson, a young woman from Scotland, had been hired years earlier to help with housework in John's farmhouse. She had known nothing about communicating with a deaf and blind person, but because she liked Helen so much, she learned quickly. Now Helen wanted Polly to accompany her on the vaudeville circuit.

This time was very difficult for Annie. Her eyes were beginning to fail her, and she was terrified of going blind.

"Helen is and always has been well behaved in her blindness, but I'm making a useless fight of it, like a bucking bronco," Annie explained. "It's not the big things in life that one misses through loss of sight, but such little things as being able to read. And I have no patience, like Helen, for the Braille system, because I can't read fast enough."

Not only was Annie worried that she was going blind; she missed Helen terribly. With a few exceptions, Helen and Teacher had been side by side for nearly 45 years.

"My own life," Annie once said, "is so interwoven with my Helen's life that I can't separate myself from her."

Finally, the vaudeville days came to an end. Anyone who had wanted to see Helen had seen her, and without Annie, the show was not as interesting. Unlike many other vaudeville performers, Helen could not make her show new or learn some new tricks. Her story was her story. Audiences became smaller and smaller until rooms were half empty. Helen knew she must find another job quickly. Although Helen and Annie had earned an amazing amount of money, neither woman was very good about saving.

"We never think about money until we haven't any," Helen and Annie admitted.

Both women loved fancy clothes, exotic vacations, and even rare and expensive dogs. Helen, in particular, enjoyed unusual and costly meals. Because Helen couldn't see or hear, her senses of smell and taste were much more sensitive. A fabulous gourmet meal was to her as beautiful music or the view of a snowcapped mountain range might be to a sighted and hearing person. But Helen also gave away significant amounts of money to the poor, friends, and charities.

And as a result, money soon became a problem again. This time, however, an opportunity arose quickly. At a Christmas gathering in 1923, a young man named Robert Irwin met Helen. Robert was the director of a new organization called the American Foundation for the Blind, or AFB. This organization hoped to increase awareness of the problems and struggles of blind people. It also hoped to raise money so that blind people could have the medical care, education, and opportunities that had long been denied to them. Most people still believed that those who were blind were helpless, useless, and even stupid. Robert Irwin wanted the AFB to help change the way Americans thought about blind people.

Robert believed that Helen could help the new organization a great deal. "Would you be interested in speaking and fundraising?" he asked Helen.

"I'm not sure," Helen replied honestly. "I've never done that before."

In truth, neither Helen nor Annie (whose health was somewhat better) thought fundraising sounded very exciting. But it was a job. Helen told Robert that she would try it for six months and see how it went. As it turned out, Helen was a natural at motivating people to both donate money to the

AFB and view the blind differently. It was a job she would keep for the rest of her life.

"Try to imagine how you would feel if you were suddenly blind today," Helen said to large crowds at fundraisers. "Picture yourself stumbling and groping at noonday as in the night, your work, your independence gone. In that dark world, wouldn't you be glad if a friend took you by the hand and said, 'Come with me and I will teach you how to do some of the things you used to do when you could see'? That is just the kind of friend the American Foundation for the Blind is going to be to all the blind in this country—if seeing people will only give it the support it must have!"

Both Annie and Polly accompanied Helen on the fundraising tours, taking turns introducing her around the country and even overseas. When the Great Depression struck in 1929, many people were suddenly very poor, and the fundraising tour slowed down a bit. Not one to sit around doing nothing, Helen wrote a second book about her life titled *Midstream: My Later Life*. This book picked up where *The Story of My Life* had left off. It became an instant national bestseller.

During all these busy years, Helen's love of the world around her and her joy at being able to continue to learn and to help others remained strong. Those who knew Helen Keller were always impressed by her positive attitude, her happiness, and her kindness. She was rarely ill-tempered, and in spite of her limitations, Helen never felt pity for herself.

"I believe it is a sacred duty to encourage ourselves and others," Helen wrote in an essay titled "Optimism." "Because no one has the right to complain of a universe which God made good."

Still, like anyone, Helen experienced sorrow. Her close friend Alexander Graham Bell had died seven years earlier. And while Helen had been all the way across the country doing a vaudeville show, she received word (right before going onstage!) that her mother had died. Helen had not even known that her mother had been ill. Yet Helen had an unusual strength that pulled her through difficult hardships again and again.

In 1936, however, Helen's optimistic spirit would face the most bitter test of Helen's life. After more than a half century of being at Helen's side, teaching her, caring for her, and loving her— Teacher was dying.

Chapter 11

"**I** am trying so hard to live for you!"

A blind Annie Sullivan groped for Helen's hand and burst into tears. Years of illness had worn Annie's body down, and now a heart condition left her unable to get out of bed. Her dimming eyes had finally failed. Now she was blind, and the darkness terrified Annie. In spite of everything, Annie still felt the need to take care of Helen.

But now, Helen took care of Teacher. She and Polly sat by Annie's bedside day and night, doing whatever they could to make Teacher's final days more comfortable. Polly read stories, and Helen tried to remember funny things that had happened to her and Annie during all their years together. But it was hard to get Annie to smile. Friends came to visit, to say goodbye, to talk about how much Annie had done for Helen.

"Thank God I gave up my life that Helen might live," Annie said to a friend during her last week of life. "God help her to live without me when I go."

On a warm evening in October, Annie was suddenly wide awake. She laughed easily at a funny story about a rodeo. Then she grasped Helen's hand and slipped into a coma. At 7:30 the next morning, at the age of 70, Annie Sullivan died. Helen was still holding her hand when she slipped away.

"A big part of my heart has just died too," Helen said later that day.

Perhaps Annie had not received as much attention and honor as she deserved during her life, but that was not true when she died. Nearly 1500 mourners gathered at her funeral service in New York City to say farewell to the remarkable Annie Sullivan. Later, Annie's ashes were placed in a container at the National Cathedral in Washington, D.C. This was an extraordinary honor. The National Cathedral was the final resting place for presidents, military heroes, and other famous public figures. Annie Sullivan was the first woman to be buried there.

"She was among the greatest teachers of all time," the Bishop of Washington, D.C., said about Annie at her service at the Cathedral. "The touch of her hand did more than illuminate the pathway of a clouded mind; it literally emancipated a soul."

Helen was sick with sorrow. She could neither eat nor sleep for days, and she told Polly, who was now at her side at all times, that she "ached all over" with sadness.

"Everything was blurred," Helen later wrote. "It seemed as if I should forever tread paths that led nowhere, climb steps that would lead to nothing, because they could not bring me to her."

Now the world watched. Would Helen be able to go on without Annie? Many people believed that Helen would give up, retreat into her old darkness of childhood and, indeed, tread paths that led nowhere.

Helen refused to let that happen. She drew on her faith to pull her through, truly believing that Teacher was now in a better place. She focused on all of the wonderful years and experiences she had had with Teacher. Then, on a trip to Europe with Polly to get away from everything for a while, Helen had the unusual sensation that Teacher was by her side. It seemed as though Teacher wanted Helen to know that everything would be all right.

"My soul was so conscious of her presence," Helen wrote, "that I could not—I would not—say that she was dead, and I do not now."

Of course, Helen knew that Annie was gone, but in so many ways Annie was still with Helen. She always would be. It helped Helen move on and continue the work of her incredible life.

Helen continued traveling everywhere, speaking and raising money for the American Foundation for the Blind. After speaking in Washington, D.C., Helen convinced Congress that the government needed to support the printing of many more Braille books for the blind. In addition, Helen helped push through regulations that made all printed Braille the same. She still recalled her panic when taking the exams to get into Radcliffe and discovering that the math exams were in a type of Braille she didn't understand well. She never wanted another blind student to feel that same panic.

Helen also met with President Franklin Roosevelt. She felt a closeness to Roosevelt, because he was also physically disabled. Like Helen, he understood what it felt like to work to overcome limitations. Roosevelt had suffered from polio as a younger man, and the disease had left his legs paralyzed. But that never made Roosevelt feel as though he was "less" or would be unable to achieve great things. He worked terribly hard to walk short distances by wearing braces on his legs and swinging his hips to make his legs move. Although Roosevelt walked awkwardly with a cane, many Americans never even realized that he spent nearly all of his time in a wheelchair.

Likewise, Roosevelt had a great deal of admiration and respect for Helen. "Anything Helen Keller is for, I am for," Roosevelt once said.

One of the things Helen worked for was including blind people in the category of "disabled" so that they could receive financial help from the government. Up until this point, blind people were more often viewed as being completely *unable*, so many Americans felt that the government should not send them disability benefits. Roosevelt agreed with Helen that this was wrong. He also agreed that blind people should have more opportunities and receive more help than they currently had. As a result, for the first time in history, programs for the blind would be funded by the government.

Other countries all over the world saw how much Helen was doing for the blind. Here was someone who could really get things done! Soon, invitations were pouring in from all over the world for Helen to come and visit and speak. Helen and Polly traveled worldwide, and everywhere they went, they were treated with great respect and kindness. In her years with the AFB, Helen visited 35 countries, bringing her message to many hundreds of huge crowds.

"The chief handicap of the blind is not blindness, but the attitude of seeing people towards them," Helen repeated from Europe to Asia. "A person who is blind never knows his hidden sources of strength until he is treated like a normal human being and encouraged to shape his own life."

Helen was particularly loved in Japan, where she gave 97 speeches in 39 cities. The Japanese people had long believed that blindness was a curse, and the idea that many cases of blindness could be easily prevented with inexpensive medicine was something brand new and very welcome.

And the Japanese were fascinated and amazed by Helen. They had never seen anything like her. People followed her as she walked through the ancient cities, calling out her name and throwing flower petals on the ground for her to walk upon. The Emperor bowed to her. Children rushed around her, grasping her hands and offering her sweets. When Helen, a great lover of all dogs, asked about the Akita, a famous Japanese dog breed, a Japanese official rushed to find an Akita to give to Helen as a gift.

Helen later referred to this dog as "an angel in fur." She went on to say, "I know I shall never feel quite the same tenderness for any other pet. The Akita dog has all the qualities that appeal to me—he is gentle, companionable, and trusty."

Today, the Akita is a popular breed in the United States—thanks to Helen. She was the very first person to bring an Akita to America.

The president of the American Foundation for the Blind felt that the AFB could not thank Helen enough. She had done more for the blind in a handful of years than anyone could have ever imagined possible. The AFB decided to provide money and care for Helen for the rest of her life. Now in her fifties, Helen was relieved and grateful. Most of all, however, she was thankful that her work was making a difference for the blind worldwide. Sometimes, Helen could not believe how her life had turned out.

"What a strange life I lead—a kind of Cinderella-life—half glitter in crystal shoes, half mice and cinders! But it is a wonderful life all the same," Helen wrote to a friend in 1936.

In 1941, after Japanese forces bombed Pearl Harbor, the United States entered World War II. Helen was disappointed that she would no longer be able to visit Japan, but she was also angry. Although she had opposed the United States' involvement in World War I, she supported the war effort now—due mostly to what she read about what was happening in Europe.

"The life-and-death quality of the Nazi violence makes me feel that it is better for all of us who uphold freedom to fight against those who murder the soul and destroy human rights," Helen wrote.

As the war progressed, President Roosevelt asked Helen if she would consider visiting wounded soldiers at military hospitals across the country. Roosevelt knew how Helen could inspire people, and he thought that perhaps she could bring some hope and optimism to these sad young men. Many of them had lost limbs and were confined to wheelchairs. Others, like Helen, had lost their hearing or their vision when grenades or bombs had blown up near them. Helen agreed to go. In six months, she visited 70 army and navy hospitals.

"Wow," one young soldier said when he met Helen and grasped her hands. "I read about you when I was in high school, but I never dreamed I'd end up blind myself."

Many of the famous people who came to speak to soldiers at hospitals said only what they thought the soldiers wanted to hear. They often said that everything would be fine and that the soldiers' lives would be back to normal in no time at all. Helen didn't say these things. She knew just how tough a journey these men had ahead of them. But this didn't mean that they could not still find joy in their lives.

"Of course you will have bitter moments," Helen told them. "I do too. Of course there will be days when you feel restless and lonely and cheated. All I can tell you is, live as much like other people as you can. Keep your life full of books and work and friends. I do—and look how well it has worked for me."

Helen danced with the soldiers, stroked their hair and faces to see what they looked like, and answered their questions as honestly as she could. Some of the men were brought to tears when they saw the strength and positive attitude of this older deaf and blind woman. If she could find happiness in her dark and silent world, so could they. As for Helen, she later said that her experience with the wounded soldiers was "the crowning experience of my life." She would never forget it. Neither would the soldiers.

***

As Helen grew older, her travels slowed down. However, the world's interest in Helen Keller seemed to speed up. In 1954, when Helen was 74, a film about her life, *The Unconquered*, was released. It featured Helen talking about her accomplishments and acting out "scenes" from her life. Some people thought the film was misleading, because it made Helen's life look mostly fun and exciting.

"The film shows the triumphant end, not the continuous struggle," a close friend of Helen's wrote. "It doesn't show the long, long hours spent over the mail or the long, long hours composing speeches, memorizing them, and practicing them."

Helen herself was not always completely happy with the way she was presented in books and film. More often than not, people thought Helen Keller was some kind of amazing saint who had no faults, because that's what they had seen or read. But Helen was as human as anyone.

"I am not a perfect being," Helen once wrote. "I have more faults than I know what to do with. I have a naughty temper. I am stubborn . . . I am naturally a fighter. I am lazy. I put off till tomorrow what I might better do today."

Nevertheless, the film *The Unconquered* was extremely popular. An entire new generation of Americans was eager to learn as much as they could about Helen. Much to Helen's surprise, the film won an Academy Award in 1955. She grasped her Oscar at the awards ceremony and waved to the cameras with her famously charming smile.

During this same time, Helen began writing a book about Annie Sullivan, which she would later title *Teacher*. The writing was very difficult for Helen as she relived all her old memories of Teacher. She had difficulty sleeping and often had vivid nightmares as she struggled with the idea that Annie had "sacrificed" most of her life for Helen. But in spite of struggling to write *Teacher*, Helen would later say that it was her favorite writing experience. And the book meant more to her than anything else she had written.

Soon after *Teacher* was published, a play named *The Miracle Worker* was presented on Broadway. The play dealt with Annie and Helen's first year together in Alabama, from Helen's "wild animal" behavior to the moment at the water pump when she finally understood W-A-T-E-R. The play was so well liked that it was made into a movie three years later and won two Academy Awards. The twelve-year-old actress Patty Duke, who played the young Helen in the movie, was thrilled to meet the real Helen Keller, who was 80 at the time.

"She was so jolly!" Patty recalled. "I'd expected serious or sweet, but not jolly. Not someone who loved to laugh out loud about everything."

In 1961, Helen was having lunch with friends when, all of a sudden, she placed her hand on her forehead.

"I feel funny," she announced.

Helen had had a stroke. For the final six years of her life, Helen had to stay in her home in Connecticut. But in many ways, Helen was happy to finally have all the time she wanted to read, sit in her garden, and spend time with her beloved dogs. For many years, her life had been in constant motion. It was nice to be still.

On a warm summer evening in 1968, Helen Keller died peacefully in her sleep at the age of 87. In her final days, Helen knew she was dying. But she wasn't afraid. She truly believed she would meet Annie, her parents, and all of her dear old friends again in the next life. And right up to the end, Helen Keller never failed to look ahead with optimism, even when looking ahead meant facing death.

"Death is no more than passing from one room into another," Helen had once told Teacher with a smile. "But there's a difference for me, you know. Because in that other room I shall be able to see."